THE 1776 REPORT

The 1776 Report

WITH A PREFACE, NOTES,
AND COMMENTARY BY

*Larry P. Arnn, Carol Swain,
and Matthew Spalding*

ENCOUNTER BOOKS   NEW YORK · LONDON

First American edition published in 2021 by Encounter Books,
an activity of Encounter for Culture and Education, Inc.,
a nonprofit, tax-exempt corporation.
Encounter Books website address: www.encounterbooks.com

Manufactured in the United States and printed on
acid-free paper. The paper used in this publication meets
the minimum requirements of ANSI/NISO Z39.48-1992
(R 1997) (*Permanence of Paper*).

FIRST AMERICAN EDITION

LIBRARY OF CONGRESS CATALOGING-IN-PUBLICATION
DATA IS AVAILABLE

TABLE OF CONTENTS

PREFACE

THE 1776 REPORT proceeds from a commission announced on Constitution Day, September 17, 2020. Its purpose was to advise the President of the United States and the nation about how to prepare for the 250th anniversary of the Declaration of Independence in July 2026.

The Commission's first responsibility was to produce a report summarizing in accurate terms the principles of the American founding and how these principles have shaped our country. Accurate and honest telling of the American story being vital to well-being and unity of the nation, the Commission was also directed to consider ways to recover and sustain an excellent teaching of American history.

While we are partisans of the cause of our country, this report is not a partisan effort. Most of the history set forth in this report enjoys broad agreement among scholars. Our task was to summarize that history, make note of some contentious issues, and ponder how the story of the American Founding might be best taught to our students. We composed this report and submitted it to one president with the full intent to advise that one, or the next, whatever might come.

We offered *The 1776 Report* to a deeply divided nation. Our divisions today are not so grave as the worst, which came in the American Revolution and again in the Civil War, but as in those times we differ greatly about the central meaning of our nation. And because the principles of the nation make claims about the nature of human beings and about human liberty, we are arguing today about the basis of everything human.

The principles and events of the American founding are a matter of history. The way to settle disputes about them is to examine the historical record. In that record will be found the truth about what America's founders meant, intended, and envisioned in establishing this nation. This report calls for such an examination. The purpose of studying history, like education itself, is the pursuit of truth. We today may differ from the founders very much, but that does not change what they thought and did, and to know what they thought and did provides us context and likely direction for our time.

The 1776 Report rehearses some evident and essential features of American history. It recommends that these become the framework through which American history is taught. These features include the majesty and the unique nature of the Declaration of Independence, the central document of our nation's founding that, despite its practical purposes, articulates universal principles of freedom and equality that are true for all men and all time.

They include the unsurpassed success of the Constitution of the United States, the basis of a representative form of government wherein the people are the sovereign over a government to which they have vested the authority to secure their rights according to their consent.

They also include the imperfections in and stains upon American history, small and large, especially the blight of slavery and race discrimination, and they include the obvious fact that those particular practices are condemned with eloquence and lasting fame by the Declaration of Independence.

They include the story of the greatest Americans, the ones who fought against despotism from Bunker Hill to Yorktown, who fought against slavery at Gettysburg and Cold Harbor and hundreds of other battles; against tyranny at Belleau Wood, Omaha Beach, and Pork Chop Hill. They include especially those who perished in all those battles, and in battles still today, and those yet to come.

They include those who led those soldiers and helped to inspire their sacrifices, statesmen like Washington and Lincoln, Franklin Roosevelt and Ronald Reagan; civic leaders like Frederick Douglass, Susan B. Anthony, Booker T. Washington, and Martin Luther King, Jr. They include the men and women of every color who fought to protect the rights of all. They were all, black and white, men and women, devoted to the ideals of the Declaration of Independence.

This is the story of America, one of the most consequential and inspiring stories in human history. It is the only basis upon which we can unite as a people, for it is our story. It makes us a people, and ennobles our common purpose. We should recover it, teach it, and revere it.

The 1776 Report was submitted to the President and released as a public document on January 18, 2021—Martin Luther King Jr. Day. The President's Advisory 1776 Commission was abolished by an Executive Order of the next President on Inauguration Day, January 20, 2021.

Herein is the original text of *The 1776 Report*, with the addition of footnotes and some explanatory commentary to support our work. It was written not for professional historians as much as for the American people. We intend it to inform but also to inspire. We encourage you to read it for yourself.

While a Commission can be formally dissolved, and a document may be removed from a website, these principles and our history can never be erased.

We will all—indeed, all of us must—continue to work together to perpetuate and defend these principles and the free life they protect.

I

INTRODUCTION

I N THE COURSE of human events there have always been those who deny or reject human freedom, but Americans will never falter in defending the fundamental truths of human liberty proclaimed on July 4, 1776. We will—*we must*—always hold these truths.

The declared purpose of the President's Advisory 1776 Commission is to "enable a rising generation to understand the history and principles of the founding of the United States in 1776 and to strive to form a more perfect Union." This requires a restoration of American education, which can only be grounded on a history of those principles that is "accurate, honest, unifying, inspiring, and ennobling."[1] And a rediscovery of our shared identity rooted in our founding principles is the path to a renewed American unity and a confident American future.

The Commission's first responsibility is to produce a report summarizing the principles of the American founding and how those principles have shaped our country. That can only be done by truthfully recounting the aspirations and actions of the men and women who sought to build America as a shining "city on a hill"—an exemplary nation, one that protects the safety and promotes the happiness of its people, as an example to be admired and emulated by nations of the world that wish to steer their government toward greater liberty and justice. The record of our founders' striving and the nation they built is our shared inheritance and remains a beacon, as Abraham Lincoln said, "to all men and all times."[2]

Today, however, Americans are deeply divided about the meaning of their country, its history, and how it should be governed. This division is severe enough to call to mind the disagreements between the colonists and King George, and those between the Confederate and Union forces in the Civil War. They amount to a dispute over not only the history of our country but also its present purpose and future direction.

The facts of our founding are not partisan. They are a matter of history. Controversies about the meaning of the founding can begin to be resolved by looking at the facts of our nation's founding. Properly understood, these facts address the concerns and aspirations of Americans of all social classes, income levels, races and religions, regions and walks of life. As well, these facts provide necessary—and wise—cautions against unrealistic hopes and checks against pressing partisan claims or utopian agendas too hard or too far.

The principles of the American founding can be learned by studying the abundant documents contained in the record. Read fully and carefully, they show how the American people have ever pursued freedom and justice, which are the political conditions for living well. To learn this history is to become a better person, a better citizen, and a better partner in the American experiment of self-government.

Comprising actions by imperfect human beings, the American story has its share of missteps, errors, contradictions, and

Washington Crossing the Delaware, by Emanuel Leutze (1851)
Source: The Metropolitan Museum of Art

wrongs. These wrongs have always met resistance from the clear principles of the nation, and therefore our history is far more one of self-sacrifice, courage, and nobility. America's principles are named at the outset to be both universal—applying to everyone—and eternal: existing for all time. The remarkable American story unfolds under and because of these great principles.

Of course, neither America nor any other nation has perfectly lived up to the universal truths of equality, liberty, justice, and government by consent. But no nation before America ever dared state those truths as the formal basis for its politics, and none has strived harder, or done more, to achieve them.

Lincoln aptly described the American government's fundamental principles as "a standard maxim for free society," which should be "familiar to all, and revered by all; constantly looked to, constantly labored for, and even though never perfectly attained, constantly approximated." But the very attempt to attain them—*every* attempt to attain them—would, Lincoln contin-

ued, constantly spread and deepen the influence of these principles and augment "the happiness and value of life to all people
of all colors everywhere."[3] The story of America is the story of
this ennobling struggle.

The President's Advisory 1776 Commission presents this first
report with the intention of cultivating a better education among
Americans in the principles and history of our nation and in the
hope that a rediscovery of those principles and the forms of constitutional government will lead to a more perfect Union.

II

THE MEANING OF
THE DECLARATION

THE UNITED STATES OF AMERICA is in most respects a
nation like any other. It embraces a people, who inhabit a
territory, governed by laws administered by human beings. Like
other countries, our country has borders, resources, industries,
cities and towns, farms and factories, homes, schools, and houses of worship. And, although a relatively young country, its people have shared a history of common struggle and achievement,
from carving communities out of a vast, untamed wilderness, to
winning independence and forming a new government, through
wars, industrialization, waves of immigration, technological
progress, and political change.

In other respects, however, the United States is unusual. It is
a republic; that is to say, its government was designed to be directed by the will of the people rather than the wishes of a single
individual or a narrow class of elites. Republicanism is an ancient
form of government but one uncommon throughout history, in
part because of its fragility, which has tended to make republics
short-lived. Contemporary Americans tend to forget how historically rare republicanism has been, in part because of the success

Declaration of Independence, by John Trumbull (1819)
Source: Wikimedia Commons

of republicanism in our time, which is derived in no small part from the very example and success of America.

In two decisive respects, the United States of America is unique. First, it has a definite birthday: July 4th, 1776. Second, it declares from the moment of its founding not merely the principles on which its new government will be based; it asserts those principles to be true and universal: "applicable to all men and all times," as Lincoln said.[1]

Other nations may have birthdays. For instance, what would eventually evolve into the French Republic was born in 1789 when Parisians stormed a hated prison and launched the downfall of the French monarchy and its aristocratic regime. The Peoples Republic of China was born in 1949 when Mao Tse Tung's Chinese Communist Party defeated the Nationalists in the Chinese Civil War. But France and China as nations—as peoples and cultures inhabiting specific territories—stretch back centuries and even millennia, over the course of many governments.

There was no United States of America before July 4th, 1776. There was not yet, formally speaking, an American people. There were, instead, living in the thirteen British colonies in North America some two-and-a-half million subjects of a distant king. Those subjects became a people by declaring themselves such and then by winning the independence they had asserted as their right.

They made that assertion on the basis of principle, not blood or kinship or what we today might call "ethnicity." Yet this fact must be properly understood. As John Jay explained in *Federalist 2*,

> Providence has been pleased to give this one connected country to one united people—a people descended from the same ancestors, speaking the same language, professing the same religion, attached to the same principles of government, very similar in their manners and customs, and who, by their joint counsels, arms, and efforts, fighting side by side throughout a long and bloody war, have nobly established general liberty and independence.[2]

Yet, as Jay (and all the founders) well knew, the newly-formed American people were not *quite* as homogenous—in ancestry, language, or religion—as this statement would seem to assert. They were neither wholly English nor wholly Protestant nor wholly Christian. Some other basis would have to be found and asserted to bind the new people together and to which they would remain attached if they were to remain a people. That basis was the assertion of universal and eternal principles of justice and political legitimacy.

But this too must be qualified. Note that Jay lists six factors binding the American people together, of which principle is only one—the most important or decisive one, but still only one, and insufficient by itself. The American founders understood that, for republicanism to function and endure, a republican people must share a large measure of commonality in manners, customs, language, and dedication to the common good.

All states, all governments, make some claim to legitimacy— that is, an argument for why their existence and specific form are justified. Some dismiss all such claims to legitimacy as false, advanced to fool the ruled into believing that their rulers' actions are justified when in fact those actions only serve the private interests of a few.

But no actual government understands itself this way, much less makes such a cynical claim in public. All actual governments, rather, understand themselves as just and assert a public claim as to why. At the time of the American founding, the most widespread claim was a form of the divine right of kings, that is to say, the assertion that God appoints some men, or some families, to rule and consigns the rest to be ruled.

The American founders rejected that claim. As the eighteen charges leveled against King George in the Declaration of Independence make clear, our founders considered the British government of the time to be oppressive and unjust. They had no wish to replace the arbitrary government of one tyrant with that of another.

More fundamentally, having cast off their political connection to England, our founders needed to state a new principle of political legitimacy for their new government. As the Declaration of Independence puts it, a "decent respect to the opinions of mankind" required them to explain themselves and justify their actions.

They did not merely wish to assert that they disliked British rule and so were replacing it with something they liked better. They wished to state a justification for their actions, and for the government to which it would give birth, that is both true and moral: moral because it is faithful to the truth about things.

★ ★ ★

"All honor to Jefferson—to the man who,
in the concrete pressure of a struggle for
national independence by a single people,
had the coolness, forecast, and capacity to
introduce into a merely revolutionary document,
an abstract truth, applicable to all men and
all times, and so to embalm it there, that to-day,
and in all coming days, it shall be a rebuke and
a stumbling-block to the very harbingers of
re-appearing tyranny and oppression."

—ABRAHAM LINCOLN

★ ★ ★

Such a justification could only be found in the precepts of nature—specifically human nature—accessible to the human mind but not subject to the human will. Those precepts—whether understood as created by God or simply as eternal—are a given that man did not bring into being and cannot change. Hence the

Declaration speaks of both "the Laws of Nature and of Nature's God"—it appeals to both reason and revelation—as the foundation of the underlying truth of the document's claims, and for the legitimacy of this new nation.

The core assertion of the Declaration, and the basis of the founders' political thought, is that "all men are created equal." From the principle of equality, the requirement for consent naturally follows: if all men are equal, then none may by right rule another without his consent.

The assertion that "all men are created equal" must also be properly understood. It does not mean that all human beings are equal in wisdom, courage, or any of the other virtues and talents that God and nature distribute unevenly among the human race. It means rather that human beings are equal in the sense that they are not by nature divided into castes, with natural rulers and ruled.

Thomas Jefferson liked to paraphrase the republican political thinker Algernon Sidney: "the mass of mankind has not been born with saddles on their backs, nor a favored few booted and spurred, ready to ride them legitimately, by the grace of God."[3] Superiority of talent—even a superior ability to rule—is not a divine or natural title or warrant to rule. George Washington, surely one of the ablest statesmen who ever lived, never made such an outlandish claim and, indeed, vehemently rejected such assertions made by others about him.

As Abraham Lincoln would later explain, there was no urgent need for the founders to insert into a "merely revolutionary document" this "abstract truth, applicable to all men and all times." They could simply have told the British king they were separating and left it at that. But they enlarged the

Martin Luther King, Jr. at the National Mall, Aug. 28, 1963
Source: Wikimedia Commons

scope of their Declaration so that its principles would serve as "a rebuke and a stumbling-block to the very harbingers of re-appearing tyranny and oppression."[4] The finality of the truth that "all men are created equal" was intended to make impossible any return to formal or legal inequality, whether to older forms such as absolute monarchy and hereditary aristocracy, or to as-yet-unimagined forms we have seen in more recent times.

Natural equality requires not only the consent of the governed but also the recognition of fundamental human rights—including but not limited to life, liberty, and the pursuit of happiness—as well as the fundamental duty or obligation of all to respect the rights of others. These rights are found in nature and are not created by man or government; rather, men create governments to secure natural rights. Indeed, the very purpose of government is to secure these rights, which exist independently of government, whether government recognizes them or not. A bad government may deny or ignore natural rights and even prevent their exercise in the real world. But it can never negate or eliminate them.*

The principles of the Declaration are universal and eternal. Yet they were asserted by a specific people, for a specific purpose, in a specific circumstance. The general principles stated in the document explain and justify the founders' particular actions in breaking off from Great Britain, and also explain the principles upon which they would build their new government. These principles apply to all men, but the founders acted to secure only Americans' rights, not those of all mankind. The world is still—and will always be—divided into nations, not all of which respect the rights of their people, though they should.

We confront, finally, the difficulty that the eternal principles elucidated in the Declaration were stated, and became the basis for an actual government, only a relatively short time ago. Yet if these principles are both eternal and accessible to the human mind, why were they not discovered and acted upon long before 1776?

In a sense, the precepts of the American founders were known to prior thinkers, but those thinkers stated them in entirely different terms to fit the different political and intellectual circumstances of their times. For instance, ancient philosophers

---

* This is, by no means, a partisan or controversial opinion, as attested to by then-Senator Joseph Biden, speaking as Chairman of the Senate Judiciary Committee: "As a child of God, I believe my rights are not derived from the Constitution. My rights are not derived from any government. My rights are not derived from any majority. My rights are because I exist. They were given to me and each of my fellow citizens by our creator and they represent the essence of human dignity." U.S. Congress, Senate, Committee on the Judiciary, Hearing on the Nomination of Robert H. Bork to the Supreme Court of the United States, 100th Cong., 1st sess., 1987, 97. In general, see Thomas G. West, *The Political Theory of the American Founding: Natural Rights, Public Policy, and the Moral Conditions of Freedom* (Cambridge: Cambridge University Press, 2017).

appear to teach that wisdom is a genuine title to rule and that in a decisive respect all men are not created equal. Yet they also teach that it is all but impossible for any actual, living man to attain genuine wisdom. Even if wisdom is a legitimate title to rule, if perfect wisdom is unattainable by any living man, then

★ ★ ★

"When the architects of our republic wrote the magnificent words of the Constitution and the Declaration of Independence, they were signing a promissory note to which every American was to fall heir. This note was a promise that all men, yes, black men as well as white men, would be guaranteed the unalienable rights to life, liberty, and the pursuit of happiness."
—MARTIN LUTHER KING, JR.

★ ★ ★

no man is by right the ruler of any other except by their consent.

More fundamentally, by the time of the American founding, political life in the West had undergone two momentous changes. The first was the sundering of civil from religious law with the advent and widespread adoption of Christianity. The second momentous change was the emergence of multiple denominations within Christianity that undid Christian unity and in turn greatly undermined political unity. Religious differences became sources of political conflict and war. As discussed further in Appendix II, it was in response to these fundamentally new circumstances that the American founders developed the principle of religious liberty.

While the founders' principles are both true and eternal, they cannot be understood without also understanding that they were formulated by practical men to solve real-world problems. For the founders' solution to these problems we must turn to the Constitution.

III

A CONSTITUTION OF
PRINCIPLES

I T IS ONE THING to discern and assert the true principles of political legitimacy and justice. It is quite another to establish those principles among an actual people, in an actual government, here on earth. As Winston Churchill put it in a not dissimilar context, even the best of men struggling in the most just of causes cannot guarantee victory; they can only deserve it.

The founders of the United States, perhaps miraculously, achieved what they set out to achieve. They defeated the world's strongest military and financial power and won their independence. They then faced the task of forming a country that would honor and implement the principles upon which they had declared their independence.[1]

The bedrock upon which the American political system is built is the rule of law. The vast difference between tyranny and the rule of law is a central theme of political thinkers back to classical antiquity. The idea that the law is superior to rulers is the cornerstone of English constitutional thought as it developed over the centuries. The concept was transferred to the American colonies, and can be seen expressed throughout colonial pamphlets and political writings. As Thomas Paine reflected in *Common Sense*:

> For as in absolute governments the King is law, so in free countries the law ought to be king; and there ought to be no other. But lest any ill use should afterwards arise, let the crown at the conclusion of the ceremony be demolished, and scattered among the people whose right it is.[2]

To assure such a government, Americans demanded a written legal document that would create both a structure and a process for securing their rights and liberties and spell out the divisions and limits of the powers of government. That legal document must be above ordinary legislation and day-to-day politics. That is what the founders meant by "constitution," and why our Constitution is "the supreme Law of the Land."

Their first attempt at a form of government, the Articles of Confederation and Perpetual Union, was adopted in the midst of the Revolutionary War and not ratified until 1781. During that time, American statesmen and citizens alike concluded that the Articles were too weak to fulfill a government's core functions. This consensus produced the Constitutional Convention of 1787, which met in Philadelphia that summer to write the document which we have today. It is a testament to those framers' wisdom and skill that the Constitution they produced remains the longest continually-operating written constitution in all of human history.

The meaning and purpose of the Constitution of 1787, however, cannot be understood without recourse to the principles of the Declaration of Independence—human equality, the requirement for government by consent, and the securing of natural rights—which the Constitution is intended to embody, protect, and nurture. Lincoln famously described the principles of the Declaration (borrowing from Proverbs 25:11) as an "apple of gold" and the Constitution as a "frame of silver" meant to "adorn and preserve" the apple. The latter was made for the former, not the reverse.[3]

★ ★ ★

"The safety of a republic depends essentially
on the energy of a common national sentiment;
on a uniformity of principles and habits;
on the exemption of the citizens from foreign bias,
and prejudice; and on that love of country which
will almost invariably be found to be closely
connected with birth, education and family."
—ALEXANDER HAMILTON

★ ★ ★

The form of the new government that the Constitution delineates is informed in part by the charges the Declaration levels at the British crown. For instance, the colonists charge the British king with failing to provide, or even interfering with, representative government; hence the Constitution provides for a representative legislature. It also charges the king with concentrating executive, legislative, and judicial power into the same hands, which James Madison pronounced "the very definition of tyranny."[4] Instead, the founders organized their new government into three coequal

The Preamble and First Article of the
Constitution of the United States of America (1787)
Source: National Archives and Records Administration

branches, checking and balancing the power of each against the others to reduce the risk of abuse of power.

The intent of the framers of the Constitution was to construct a government that would be sufficiently strong to perform those essential tasks that only a government can perform (such as establishing justice, ensuring domestic tranquility, providing for the common defense, and promoting the general welfare— the main tasks named in the document's preamble), but not so strong as to jeopardize the people's liberties. In other words, the new government needed to be strong enough to have the power to secure rights without having so much power as to enable or encourage it to *infringe* rights.

More specifically, the framers intended the new Constitution to keep the thirteen states *united*—to prevent the breakup of the Union into two or more smaller countries—while maintaining sufficient latitude and liberty for the individual states.

The advantages of union are detailed in the first fourteen papers of *The Federalist* (a series of essays written to urge the Constitution's adoption), and boil down to preventing and deterring foreign adventurism in North America, avoiding conflicts between threats, achieving economies of scale, and best utilizing the diverse resources of the continent.

While the Constitution is fundamentally a compact among the American people (its first seven words are "We the People of the United States"), it was ratified by special conventions in the states. The peoples of the states admired and cherished their state governments, all of which had adopted republican constitutions before a federal constitution was completed. Hence the framers of the new national government had to respect the states' prior existence and jealous guarding of their own prerogatives.

They also believed that the role of the federal government should be limited to performing those tasks that only a national government can do, such as providing for the nation's security or regulating commerce between the states, and that most tasks were properly the responsibility of the states. And they believed that strong states, as competing power centers, would act as counterweights against a potentially overweening central government, in the same way that the separation of powers checks and balances the branches of the federal government.

★ ★ ★

> "To throw obstacles in the way of a complete
> education is like putting out the eyes;
> to deny the rights of property is like cutting off
> the hands. To refuse political equality is
> to rob the ostracized of all self-respect, of credit
> in the market place, of recompense in
> the world of work, of a voice in choosing those
> who make and administer the law, a choice in
> the jury before whom they are tried, and in the
> judge who decides their punishment."
> —ELIZABETH CADY STANTON

★ ★ ★

For the founders, the principle that just government requires the consent of the governed in turn requires republicanism, because the chief way that consent is granted to a government on an ongoing basis is through the people's participation in the political process. This is the reason the Constitution "guarantee[s] to every State in this Union a Republican Form of Government."

Under the United States Constitution, the people are sovereign. But the people do not directly exercise their sovereignty, for instance, by voting directly in popular assemblies. Rather, they do so indirectly, through representative institutions. This is, on the most basic level, a practical requirement in a republic with a large population and extent of territory. But it is also intended to be a remedy to the defects common to all republics up to that time.

The framers of the Constitution faced a twofold challenge. They had to assure those alarmed by the historical record that the new government was not *too republican* in simply copying the old, failed forms, while also reassuring those concerned about overweening centralized power that the government of the new Constitution was republican enough to secure equal natural rights and prevent the reemergence of tyranny.

The main causes of prior republican failure were class conflict and tyranny of the majority. In the simplest terms, the largest single faction in any republic would tend to band together and unwisely wield their numerical strength against unpopular minorities, leading to conflict and eventual collapse. The founders' primary remedy was union itself. Against the old idea that republics had to be small, the founders countered that the very smallness of prior republics all but guaranteed their failure. In small republics, the majority can more easily organize itself into a dominant faction; in large republics, interests become too numerous for any single faction to dominate.

The inherent or potential partisan unwisdom of a dominant faction also would be tempered by representative government. Rather than the people acting as a body, the people would instead select officeholders to represent them. This would refine and enlarge the public views, by passing them through the medium of a chosen body of citizens, whose wisdom may best discern the true interest of their country, and whose patriotism and love of justice will be least likely to sacrifice it to temporary or partial considerations.[5]

And the separation of powers would work in concert with the principle of representation by incentivizing individual officeholders to identify their personal interests with the powers and prerogatives of their offices, and thus keep them alert to the danger of encroachments from other branches and offices.

The founders asserted that these innovations, and others, combined to create a republicanism that was at once old as well as new: true to the eternal principles and timeless ends of good government, but awake to and corrective of the deficiencies in prior examples of popular rule.

One important feature of our written constitution is the careful way that it *limits* the powers of each branch of government—that is, states what those branches may do, and by implication what they may *not* do. This is the real meaning of "limited government": not that the government's size or funding levels remain small, but that government's powers and activities must remain limited to certain carefully defined areas and responsibilities as guarded by bicameralism, federalism, and the separation of powers.

The Constitution was intended to endure. But because the founders well knew that no document written by human beings could ever be perfect or anticipate every future contingency, they provided for a process to amend the document—but only

Frederick Douglass in Hillsdale, Michigan, January 1863
Source: Hillsdale College

by popular decision-making and not by ordinary legislation or judicial decree.

The first ten amendments, which would come to be known as the Bill of Rights, were included at the demand of those especially concerned about vesting the federal government with too much power and who wanted an enumeration of specific rights that the new government lawfully could not transgress.

★ ★ ★

"Freedom is never more than one generation away from extinction. We didn't pass it to our children in the bloodstream. It must be fought for, protected, and handed on for them to do the same, or one day we will spend our sunset years telling our children and our children's children what it was once like in the United States where men were free."

—RONALD REAGAN

★ ★ ★

But all agreed that substantive rights are not granted by government; any just government exists only to secure these rights. And they specifically noted in the Ninth Amendment that the Bill of Rights was a selective and not an exclusive list; that is, the mere fact that a right is not mentioned in the Bill of Rights is neither proof nor evidence that it does not exist.

It is important to note the founders' understanding of three of these rights that are decisive for republican government and the success of the founders' project.

Our first freedom, religious liberty, is foremost a moral requirement of the natural freedom of the human mind. As discussed in Appendix II, it is also the indispensable solution to the political-religious problem that emerged in the modern world. Faith is both a matter of private conscience and public import, which is why the founders encouraged religious free exercise but barred the government from establishing any one national religion. The point is not merely to protect the state from religion but also to protect religion from the state so that religious institutions would flourish and pursue their divine mission among men.

Like religious liberty, freedom of speech and of the press is required by the freedom of the human mind. More plainly, it is a requirement for any government in which the people choose the direction of government policy. To choose requires public deliberation and debate. A people that cannot publicly express its opinions, exchange ideas, or openly argue about the course of its government is not free.

Finally, the right to keep and bear arms is required by the fundamental natural right to life: no man may justly be denied the means of his own defense. The political significance of this right is hardly less important. An armed people is a people capable of defending their liberty no less than their lives and is the last, desperate check against the worst tyranny.

IV

CHALLENGES TO
AMERICA'S PRINCIPLES

C HALLENGES to constitutional government are frequent and
to be expected in a popular government based on consent.
In his Farewell Address, George Washington advised his coun-
trymen that when it came to the preservation of the Constitution they should "resist with care the spirit of innovation upon its
principles however specious the pretexts."[1] The Constitution has
proven sturdy against narrow interest groups that seek to change
elements of the Constitution merely to get their way.

At the same time, it is important to note that by design
there is room in the Constitution for significant change and reform. Indeed, great reforms—like abolition, women's suffrage,
anti-Communism, the Civil Rights Movement, and the Pro-
Life Movement—have often come forward that improve our
dedication to the principles of the Declaration of Independence
under the Constitution.

More problematic have been movements that reject the fundamental truths of the Declaration of Independence and seek to destroy our constitutional order. The arguments, tactics, and names
of these movements have changed, and the magnitude of the chal-

lenge has varied, yet they are all united by adherence to the same falsehood—that people do not have equal worth and equal rights.

At the infancy of our Republic, the threat was a despotic king who violated the people's rights and overthrew the colonists' long-standing tradition of self-government. After decades of struggle, the colonists succeeded in establishing a more perfect Union founded not upon the capricious whims of a tyrant, but republican laws and institutions founded upon self-evident and eternal truths.

It is the sacred duty of every generation of American patriots to defend this priceless inheritance.

Slavery

The most common charge levelled against the founders, and hence against our country itself, is that they were hypocrites who didn't believe in their stated principles, and therefore the country they built rests on a lie. This charge is untrue, and has done enormous damage, especially in recent years, with a devastating effect on our civic unity and social fabric.*

---

* "On the American Revolution, pivotal to any account of our history, the [1619] project asserts that the founders declared the colonies' independence of Britain 'in order to ensure slavery would continue.' This is not true. If supportable, the allegation would be astounding—yet every statement offered by the project to validate it is false." Victoria Bynum, James M. McPherson, James Oakes, Sean Wilentz, Gordon S. Wood, Letter to the Editor, *New York Times*, December 20, 2019, https://www.nytimes.com/2019/12/20/magazine/we-respond-to-the-historians-who-critiqued-the-1619-project.html. "No insincerity or hypocrisy can fairly be laid to their charge. Never, from their lips, was heard one syllable of attempt to justify the institution of slavery. They universally considered it as a reproach fastened upon them by the unnatural step-mother country; and they saw that, before the principles of the Declaration of Independence, slavery, in common with every other mode of oppression, was destined sooner or later to be banished from the earth. Such was the undoubting conviction of Jefferson to his dying day." John

Many Americans labor under the illusion that slavery was somehow a uniquely American evil. It is essential to insist at the outset that the institution be seen in a much broader perspective. It is very hard for people brought up in the comforts of modern America, in a time in which the idea that all human beings have inviolable rights and inherent dignity is almost taken for granted, to imagine the cruelties and enormities that were endemic in earlier times. But the unfortunate fact is that the institution of slavery has been more the rule than the exception throughout human history.[2]

It was the Western world's repudiation of slavery, only just beginning to build at the time of the American Revolution, which marked a dramatic sea change in moral sensibilities.[3] The American founders were living on the cusp of this change, in a manner that straddled two worlds. George Washington owned slaves, but came to detest the practice, and wished for "a plan adopted for the abolition of it."[4] By the end of his life, he freed all the slaves in his family estate.

Thomas Jefferson also held slaves, and yet included in his original draft of the Declaration a strong condemnation of slavery, which was removed at the insistence of certain slaveholding delegates.[5] Inscribed in marble at his memorial in Washington, D.C. is Jefferson's foreboding reference to the injustice of slavery: "I tremble for my country when I reflect that God is just; that His justice cannot sleep forever."[6]

James Madison saw to it at the Constitutional Convention that, even when the Constitution compromised with slavery, it

Quincy Adams, An Oration Delivered Before the Inhabitants of the Town of Newburyport at Their Request, on the Sixty-First Anniversary of the Declaration of Independence, July 4th, 1837, (Newburyport, MA: Morss & Brewster, 1837), 50.

Portrait of Abraham Lincoln taken by Alexander Gardner, Nov. 8, 1863
Source: Wikimedia Commons

never used the word "slave" to do so. No mere semantics, he insisted that it was "wrong to admit in the Constitution the idea that there could be property in men."[7]

Indeed, the compromises at the Constitutional Convention

were just that: compromises. The three-fifths compromise was proposed by an antislavery delegate to prevent the South from counting their slaves as whole persons for purposes of increasing their congressional representation. The so-called fugitive slave clause, perhaps the most hated protection of all, accommodated pro-slavery delegates but was written so that the Constitution did not sanction slavery in the states where it existed. There is also the provision in the Constitution that forbade any restriction of the slave trade for twenty years after ratification—at which time Congress immediately outlawed the slave trade.*

The First Continental Congress agreed to discontinue the slave trade and boycott other nations that engaged in it, and the Sec-

---

* On the Constitution and slavery, see Don E. Fehrenbacher, *The Slaveholding Republic: An Account of the United States Government's Relations to Slavery* (New York: Oxford University Press, 2001), 29-47. Fehrenbacher concludes: "In short, the Constitution as it came from the hands of the framers dealt only minimally and peripherally with slavery and was essentially open-ended on the subject. Nevertheless, because it substantially increased the power of the national government, the Constitution had greater proslavery potential and greater antislavery potential than the Articles of Confederation. Its meaning with respect to slavery would depend heavily upon how it was implemented." Likewise, Sean Wilentz concludes: "In hindsight, the slaveholders' victories can look utterly one-sided and forbidding, just as northern critics and southern supporters of the Constitution at the time claimed they were. Judging from what we now know about what happened in Philadelphia, though, the Constitution's proslavery features appear substantial but incomplete. Above all, the convention took care to prevent the Constitution from recognizing what had become slavery's main legal and political bulwark during the northern struggles over emancipation, the legitimacy of property in man. While they had no choice in the moment but to tolerate and even protect slavery where it existed, they would prepare for a nation in which there was no slavery, which would mean refusing to validate slavery's legitimacy in the Constitution. And during the decades to come, that exclusion proved the Achilles' heel of proslavery politics." Sean Wilentz, *No Property in Man: Slavery and Antislavery at the Nation's Founding* (Cambridge: Harvard University Press, 2018), 59.

ond Continental Congress reaffirmed this policy.[8] The Northwest Ordinance, a pre-Constitution law passed to govern the western territories (and passed again by the First Congress and signed into law by President Washington) explicitly bans slavery from those territories and from any states that might be organized there.[9]

Above all, there is the clear language of the Declaration itself: "We hold these truths to be self-evident, that all men are created equal." The founders knew slavery was incompatible with *that* truth.

It is important to remember that, as a question of practical politics, no durable union could have been formed without a compromise among the states on the issue of slavery. Is it reasonable to believe that slavery could have been abolished sooner had the slave states not been in a union with the free? Perhaps. But what is momentous is that a people that included slaveholders founded their nation on the proposition that "all men are created equal."[†]

So why did they say that without immediately abolishing slavery? To establish the principle of consent as the ground of all political legitimacy and to check against any possible future drift toward or return to despotism, for sure. But also, in Lin-

† "To note only that certain leaders of the Revolution continued to enjoy the profits of so savage an institution and in their reforms failed to obliterate it inverts the propositions of the story. What is significant in the historical context of the time is not that the liberty-loving Revolutionaries allowed slavery to survive, but that they—even those who profited directly from the institution—went so far in condemning it, confining it, and setting in motion the forces that would ultimately destroy it.... A successful and liberty-loving republic might someday destroy the slavery that it had been obliged to tolerate at the start; a weak and fragmented nation would never be able to do so." Bernard Bailyn, *Faces of the Revolution: Personalities and Themes in the Struggle for American Independence* (New York: Knopf, 1990), 222-23.

coln's words, "to declare the right, so that the enforcement of it might follow as fast as circumstances should permit."[10]

The foundation of our Republic planted the seeds of the death of slavery in America. The Declaration's unqualified proclamation of human equality flatly contradicted the existence of human bondage and, along with the Constitution's compromises understood in light of that proposition, set the stage for abolition. Indeed, the movement to abolish slavery *that first began in the United States* led the way in bringing about the end of legal slavery.*

Benjamin Franklin was president of the Pennsylvania Society for Promoting the Abolition of Slavery, and John Jay (the first Chief Justice of the Supreme Court) was the president of a similar society in New York. John Adams opposed slavery his entire life as a "foul contagion in the human character" and "an evil of colossal magnitude."[11]

Frederick Douglass had been born a slave, but escaped and eventually became a prominent spokesman for the abolitionist movement. He initially condemned the Constitution, but after studying its history came to insist that it was a "glorious liberty document" and that the Declaration of Independence was "the ring-bolt to the chain of your nation's destiny."[12]

* "The Revolution almost overnight made slavery a problem in ways that it had not been earlier. The contradiction between the appeal to liberty and the existence of slavery became obvious to all the Revolutionary leaders.... Given the mounting sense of inconsistency between the Revolutionary ideals and the holding of people in bondage, it is not surprising that the first anti-slave convention in the world was held in Philadelphia in 1775. Everywhere in the country most of the Revolutionary leaders assumed that slavery was on its last legs and was headed for eventual destruction.... Perhaps the main reason many were persuaded that slavery was on its way to extinction was the widespread enthusiasm throughout America for ending the despicable slave trade." Gordon S. Wood, *Empire of Liberty: A History of the Early Republic, 1789-1815* (New York: Oxford University Press, 2009/2011), 517-18, 523.

And yet over the course of the first half of the 19th century, a growing number of Americans increasingly denied the truth at the heart of the founding. Senator John C. Calhoun of South Carolina famously rejected the Declaration's principle of equality as "the most dangerous of all political error" and a "self-evident lie." He never doubted that the founders meant what they said.[13]

★ ★ ★

"We live in an age of science and of abounding
accumulation of material things. These did not create
our Declaration. Our Declaration created them.
The things of the spirit come first. Unless we cling
to that, all our material prosperity,
overwhelming though it may appear,
will turn to a barren scepter in our grasp."

—CALVIN COOLIDGE

★ ★ ★

To this rejection, Calhoun added a new theory in which rights inhere not in every individual by "the Laws of Nature and of Nature's God" but in groups or races according to historical evolution. This new theory was developed to protect slavery— Calhoun claimed it was a "positive good"[14]—and specifically to prevent lawful majorities from stopping the spread of slavery into federal territories where it did not yet exist.

"In the way our Fathers originally left the slavery question, the institution was in the course of ultimate extinction, and the public mind rested in the belief that it was in the course of ultimate extinction," Abraham Lincoln observed in 1858. "All I have asked or desired anywhere, is that it should be placed back again upon the basis that the Fathers of our government originally placed it upon."[15]

This conflict was resolved, but at a cost of more than 600,000 lives. Constitutional amendments were passed to abolish slavery, grant equal protection under the law, and guarantee the right to vote regardless of race.[16] Yet the damage done by the denial of core American principles and by the attempted substitution of a theory of group rights in their place proved widespread and long-lasting. These, indeed, are the direct ancestors of some of the destructive theories that today divide our people and tear at the fabric of our country.

Progressivism

In the decades that followed the Civil War, in response to the industrial revolution and the expansion of urban society, many American elites adopted a series of ideas to address these changes called Progressivism. Although not all of one piece, and not without its practical merits, the political thought of Progressivism held that the times had moved far beyond the founding era, and that contemporary society was too complex any longer to be governed by principles formulated in the 18th century. To use a contemporary analogy, Progressives believed that America's original "software"—the founding documents—were no longer capable of operating America's vastly more complex "hardware": the advanced industrial society that had emerged since the founding.

More significantly, the Progressives held that truths were not permanent but only relative to their time. They rejected the self-evident truth of the Declaration that all men are created equal and are endowed equally, either by nature or by God, with unchanging rights. As one prominent Progressive historian wrote in 1922, "To ask whether the natural rights philosophy of the Declaration of Independence is true or false, is essentially a meaningless question."[17] Instead, Progressives believed there were only group rights that are constantly redefined and change with the times. Indeed, society has the power and obligation not only to define and grant new rights, but also to take old rights away as the country develops.

★ ★ ★

"Hold on, my friends, to the Constitution
and to the Republic for which it stands.
Miracles do not cluster, and what has happened
once in 6,000 years, may not happen again.
Hold on to the Constitution, because if the
American Constitution should fail, there will be
anarchy throughout the world."
—DANIEL WEBSTER

★ ★ ★

Based on this false understanding of rights, the Progressives designed a new system of government. Instead of securing fundamental rights grounded in nature, government—operating under a new theory of the "living" Constitution—should constantly evolve to secure evolving rights.

In order to keep up with these changes, government would be run more and more by credentialed managers, who would direct society through rules and regulations that mold to the currents of the time. Before he became President of the United States, Woodrow Wilson laid out this new system whereby "the functions of government are in a very real sense independent of legislation, and even constitutions," meaning that this new view of government would operate independent of the people.*

Far from creating an omniscient body of civil servants led only by "pragmatism" or "science," though, progressives instead created what amounts to a fourth branch of government called at times the bureaucracy or the administrative state. This shadow government never faces elections and today operates largely without checks and balances.[18] The founders always opposed government unaccountable to the people and without constitutional restraint, yet it continues to grow around us.

Fascism

The principles of the Declaration have been threatened not only at home. In the 20th century, two global movements threatened

* The claim here is not that progressivism is akin to slavery or fascism, but that its intellectual grounding is just as much a denial of the Declaration's principles. Woodrow Wilson, "Notes for Lectures," in *The Papers of Woodrow Wilson*, vol 7., ed. Arthur S. Link (Princeton, N.J.: Princeton University Press, 1966-1993), 121. Wilson argued that popular politics should be separated from administration and that the real decisions of governing should be made by unelected administrators immune from politics, and noted that his understanding of democracy was little different from socialism: "It is very clear that in fundamental theory socialism and democracy are almost if not quite one and the same. They both rest at bottom upon the absolute right of the community to determine its own destiny and that of its members. Men as communities are supreme over men as individuals. Limits of wisdom and convenience to the public control there may be: limits of principle there are, upon strict analysis, none." Woodrow Wilson, "Socialism and Democracy," August 22, 1887, in *The Papers of Woodrow Wilson*, Arthur S. Link, ed. vol. 5 (Princeton, NJ: Princeton University Press, 1966-1993), 559-62.

to destroy freedom and subject mankind to a new slavery. Though ideological cousins, the forces of Fascism and Communism were bitter enemies in their wars to achieve world domination. What united both totalitarian movements was their utter disdain for natural rights and free peoples.

Fascism first arose in Italy under the dictatorship of Benito Mussolini, largely in response to the rise of Bolshevism in Russia. Like the Progressives, Mussolini sought to centralize power under the management of so-called experts. All power—corporate and political—would be exercised by the state and directed toward the same goal. Individual rights and freedoms hold no purchase under Fascism. Its principle is instead, in Mussolini's words, "everything in the State, nothing outside the State, nothing against the State."[19] Eventually, Adolf Hitler in Germany wed this militant and dehumanizing political movement to his pseudo-scientific theory of Aryan racial supremacy, and Nazism was born.

The Nazi juggernaut quickly conquered much of Europe. The rule of the Axis Powers "is not a government based upon the consent of the governed," said President Franklin Delano Roosevelt. "It is not a union of ordinary, self-respecting men and women to protect themselves and their freedom and their dignity from oppression. It is an unholy alliance of power and pelf to dominate and enslave the human race."[20]

Before the Nazis could threaten America in our own hemisphere, the United States built an arsenal of democracy, creating more ships, planes, tanks, and munitions than any other power on earth. Eventually, America rose up, sending millions of troops across the oceans to preserve freedom.

Everywhere American troops went, they embodied in their own ranks and brought with them the principles of the Declaration, liberating peoples and restoring freedom. Yet, while Fascism died in 1945 with the collapse of the Axis powers, it was quickly replaced by a new threat, and the rest of the 20th century was defined by the United States' mortal and moral battle against the forces of Communism.

Communism

Communism seems to preach a radical or extreme form of human equality. But at its core, wrote Karl Marx, is "the idea of the class struggle as the immediate driving force of history, and particularly the class struggle between the bourgeois and the proletariat."[21] In the communist mind, people are not born equal and free, they are defined entirely by their class.

Under Communism, the purpose of government is not to secure rights at all. Instead, the goal is for a "class struggle [that] necessarily leads to the dictatorship of the proletariat."[22] By its very nature, this class struggle would be violent. "The Communists disdain to conceal their views and aims," Marx wrote. "They openly declare that their ends can be attained only by the forcible overthrow of all existing social conditions. Let the ruling classes tremble at a communist revolution."[23]

This radical rejection of human dignity spread throughout much of the world. In Russia, the bloody Bolshevik Revolution during World War I established the communist Soviet Union. Communism understands itself as a universalist movement of global conquest, and communist dictatorships eventually seized power through much of Europe and Asia, and in significant parts of Africa and South America.

Led by the Soviet Union, Communism even threatened, or

Ronald Reagan at the Brandenburg Gate in West Berlin, June 12, 1987
Source: Wikimedia Commons

aspired to threaten, our liberties here at home. What it could not achieve through force of arms, it attempted through subversion. Communism did not succeed in fomenting revolution in America. But Communism's relentless anti-American, anti-Western, and atheistic propaganda did inspire thousands, and perhaps millions, to reject and despise the principles of our founding and our government. While America and its allies eventually won the Cold War, this legacy of anti-Americanism is by no means entirely a memory but still pervades much of academia and the intellectual and cultural spheres. The increasingly accepted economic theory of Socialism, while less violent than Communism, is inspired by the same flawed philosophy and leads down the same dangerous path of allowing the state to seize private property and redistribute wealth as the governing elite see fit.

For generations, America stood as a bulwark against global Communism. Our Cold War victory was owing not only to our superior technology, economy, and military. In the end, America won because the Soviet Union was built upon a lie. As President Ronald Reagan said, "I have seen the rise of Fascism and Communism.... But both theories fail. Both deny those God-given liberties that are the inalienable right of each person on this planet; indeed they deny the existence of God."[24]

Racism and Identity Politics

The Thirteenth Amendment to the Constitution, passed after the Civil War, brought an end to legal slavery. Blacks enjoyed a new equality and freedom, voting for and holding elective office in states across the Union. But it did not bring an end to racism, or to the unequal treatment of blacks everywhere.

Despite the determined efforts of the postwar Reconstruction Congress to establish civil equality for freed slaves, the postbellum South ended up devolving into a system that was hardly better than slavery. The system enmeshed freedmen in relationships of extreme dependency, and used poll taxes, literacy tests, and the violence of vigilante groups like the Ku Klux Klan to prevent them from exercising their civil rights, particularly the right to vote. Jim Crow laws enforced the strict segregation of the races, and gave legal standing in some states to a pervasive subordination of blacks.[25]

It would take a national movement composed of people from different races, ethnicities, nationalities, and religions to bring about an America fully committed to ending legal discrimination. The Civil Rights Movement culminated in the 1960s with the passage of three major legislative reforms affecting segregation, voting, and housing rights. It presented itself, and was understood by the American people, as consistent with the principles of the founding.* "When the architects of our republic wrote the magnificent words of the Constitution and the Declaration of Independence, they were signing a promissory note to which every American was to fall heir," Martin Luther King, Jr. said in his "I Have a Dream" speech. "This note was a promise that all men, yes, black men as well as white men, would be guaranteed the unalienable rights to life, liberty, and the pursuit of happiness."[26]

It seemed, finally, that America's nearly two-century effort to realize fully the principles of the Declaration had reached a culmination. But the heady spirit of the original Civil Rights Movement, whose leaders forcefully quoted the Declaration of

---

* "[A] careful reading of the basic documents of the civil rights movement shows that much of the movement was conservative and backward looking. At least in its earliest stages, and to a significant extent thereafter, its defining aspirations came from America's own stated ideals. Often participants in the movement attempted to identify those ideals and to insist that the nation should live up to them." Cass R. Sunstein, "What the Civil Rights Movement Was and Wasn't," *University of Illinois Law Review* 1995, no. 1 (1995): 191-210.

Martin Luther King Jr. during the Civil Rights March on
Washington, D.C., Aug. 28, 1963
Source: National Archives

Independence, the Constitution, and the rhetoric of the founders and of Lincoln, proved to be short-lived.

The Civil Rights Movement was almost immediately turned
to programs that ran counter to the lofty ideals of the founders.
The ideas that drove this change had been growing in America
for decades, and they distorted many areas of policy in the half
century that followed. Among the distortions was the abandon-
ment of nondiscrimination and equal opportunity in favor of
"group rights" not unlike those advanced by Calhoun and his followers. The justification for reversing the promise of color-blind
civil rights was that past discrimination requires present effort,
or affirmative action in the form of preferential treatment, to

overcome long-accrued inequalities.[27] Those forms of preferential treatment built up in our system over time, first in administrative rulings, then executive orders, later in congressionally passed law, and finally were sanctified by the Supreme Court.

Today, far from a regime of equal natural rights for equal citizens, enforced by the equal application of law, we have moved toward a system of explicit group privilege that, in the name of "social justice," demands equal results and explicitly sorts citizens into "protected classes" based on race and other demographic categories.

Eventually this regime of formal inequality would come to be known as "identity politics." The stepchild of earlier rejections of the founding, identity politics (discussed in Appendix III) values people by characteristics like race, sex, and sexual orientation and holds that new times demand new rights to replace the old. This is the opposite of King's hope that his children would "live in a nation where they will not be judged by the color of their skin but by the content of their character," and denies that all are endowed with the unalienable rights to life, liberty, and the pursuit of happiness.[28]

Identity politics makes it less likely that racial reconciliation and healing can be attained by pursuing Martin Luther King, Jr.'s dream for America and upholding the highest ideals of our Constitution and our Declaration of Independence.

V

THE TASK OF
NATIONAL RENEWAL

ALL THE GOOD THINGS we see around us—from the physical infrastructure, to our high standards of living, to our exceptional freedoms—are direct results of America's unity, stability, and justice, all of which in turn rest on the bedrock of our founding principles. Yet today our country is in danger of throwing this inheritance away.

The choice before us now is clear. Will we choose the truths of the Declaration? Or will we fall prey to the false theories that have led too many nations to tyranny? It is our mission—all of us—to restore our national unity by rekindling a brave and honest love for our country and by raising new generations of citizens who not only know the self-evident truths of our founding, but act worthy of them.

This great project of national renewal depends upon true education—not merely training in particular skills, but the formation of citizens. To remain a free people, we must have the knowledge, strength, and virtue of a free people. From families and schools to popular culture and public policy, we must teach our founding principles and the character necessary to live out those principles.

This includes restoring patriotic education that teaches the truth about America. That doesn't mean ignoring the faults in our past, but rather viewing our history clearly and wholly, with reverence and love. We must also prioritize personal responsibility and fulfilling the duties we have toward one another as citizens. Above all, we must stand up to the petty tyrants in every sphere who demand that we speak only of America's sins while denying her greatness. At home, in school, at the workplace, and in the world, it is the people—and only the people—who have the power to stand up for America and defend our way of life.

The Role of the Family

By their very nature, families are the first educators, teaching children how to treat others with respect, make wise decisions, exercise patience, think for themselves, and steadfastly guard their God-given liberties. It is good mothers and fathers, above all others, who form good people and good citizens.

This is why America's founding fathers often echoed the great Roman statesman Cicero in referring to the family as the "seminary of the republic."* They understood that the habits

---

* "The primary society is in marriage itself; next is the bond of parents with their children; then one home, with all things in common; this, then, is the principle element of one's city and a kind of seminary of the republic." The Latin is taken from Cicero, *De Officiis*, trans. Walter Miller, Loeb Classical Library (Cambridge: Harvard University Press, 1913), 56. The English translation is original to this report. Citing Cicero, American Founder James Wilson wrote: "It is the principle of the community; it is that seminary, on which the commonwealth, for its manners as well as for its numbers, must ultimately depend." James Wilson, *The Works of James Wilson*, ed. Robert Green McCloskey, vol. 2, (Cambridge, Massachusetts: Belknap Press of Harvard University Press, 1967), 608.

and morals shaped in the home determine the character of our communities and the ultimate fate of our country.

When children see their mother and father hard at work, they learn the dignity of labor and the reward of self-discipline. When adults speak out against dangerous doctrines that threaten our freedoms and values, children learn the time-tested concept of free expression and the courageous spirit of American independence. When parents serve a neighbor in need, they model charity and prove that every human being has inherent worth. And when families pray together, they acknowledge together the providence of the Almighty God who gave them their sacred liberty.

For the American republic to endure, families must remain strong and reclaim their duty to raise up morally responsible citizens who love America and embrace the gifts and responsibilities of freedom and self-government.

Teaching America

The primary duty of schools is to teach students the basic skills needed to function in society, such as reading, writing, and mathematics. As discussed in Appendix IV, our founders also recognized a second and essential task: educators must convey a sense of enlightened patriotism that equips each generation with a knowledge of America's founding principles, a deep reverence for their liberties, and a profound love of their country.

Make no mistake: The love we are talking about is something different from romantic or familial love, something that cannot be imposed by teachers or schools or government edicts, least of all in a free country. Like any love worthy of the name, it must be embraced freely and be strong and unsentimental enough to coexist with the elements of disappointment, criticism, dissent, opposition, and even shame that come with moral maturity and open eyes. But it is love all the same, and without the deep foundation it supplies, our republic will perish.[1]

★ ★ ★

"Promote, then, as an object of primary
importance, institutions for the general
diffusion of knowledge. In proportion as the
structure of a government gives force
to public opinion, it is essential that
public opinion should be enlightened."
—GEORGE WASHINGTON

★ ★ ★

State and local governments—not the federal government—are responsible for adopting curricula that teach children the principles that unite, inspire, and ennoble all Americans. This includes lessons on the Revolutionary War, the Declaration of Independence, and the Constitutional Convention. Educators should teach an accurate history of how the permanent principles of America's founding have been challenged and preserved since 1776. By studying America's true heritage, students learn to embrace and preserve the triumphs of their forefathers while identifying and avoiding their mistakes.

States and school districts should reject any curriculum that promotes one-sided partisan opinions, activist propaganda, or factional ideologies that demean America's heritage, dishonor our heroes, or deny our principles. Any time teachers or administrators promote political agendas in the classroom, they abuse their platform and dishonor every family who trusts them with their children's education and moral development.

★ ★ ★

"To place before mankind the common sense of
the subject, in terms so plain and firm as to
command their assent, and to justify ourselves in
the independent stand we are compelled to take. . . .
it was intended to be an expression of the
American mind, and to give to that expression
the proper tone and spirit called for by the occasion."
—THOMAS JEFFERSON

★ ★ ★

"Law and liberty cannot rationally become the object of our love," wrote founding father James Wilson, "unless they first become the objects of our knowledge."[2] Students who are taught to understand America's exceptional principles and America's powerful history grow into strong citizens who respect the rule of law and protect the country they know and love.

A Scholarship of Freedom

Universities in the United States are often today hotbeds of anti-Americanism, libel, and censorship that combine to generate in students and in the broader culture at the very least disdain and at worst outright hatred for this country.

The founders insisted that universities should be at the core of preserving American republicanism by instructing students and future leaders of its true basis and instilling in them not just an understanding but a reverence for its principles and core documents.* Today, our higher education system does almost the precise opposite. Colleges peddle resentment and contempt for American principles and history alike, in the process weakening attachment to our shared heritage.

In order to build up a healthy, united citizenry, scholars, students, and all Americans must reject false and fashionable ideologies that obscure facts, ignore historical context, and tell America's story solely as one of oppression and victimhood rather than one of imperfection but also unprecedented achievement toward freedom, happiness, and fairness for all. Historical revisionism that tramples honest scholarship and historical truth, shames Americans by highlighting only the sins of their ancestors, and teaches claims of systemic racism that can only be eliminated by

---

* The civic object of higher education, according to Thomas Jefferson and James Madison, is "to form the statesmen, legislators and judges, on whom public prosperity and individual happiness are so much to depend; To expound the principles and structure of government, the laws which regulate the intercourse of nations, those formed municipally for our own government, and a sound spirit of legislation, which, banishing all arbitrary and unnecessary restraint on individual action, shall leave us free to do whatever does not violate the equal rights of another." See "Report of the Board of Commissioners for the University of Virginia to the Virginia General Assembly," August 4, 1818 in *The Papers of James Madison*, Retirement Series, vol. 1, 4 March 1817–31 and January 1820, ed. David B. Mattern, J. C. A. Stagg, Mary Parke Johnson, and Anne Mandeville Colony (Charlottesville: University of Virginia Press, 2013), 326–340.

more discrimination, is an ideology intended to manipulate opinions more than educate minds.

Deliberately destructive scholarship shatters the civic bonds that unite all Americans. It silences the discourse essential to a free society by breeding division, distrust, and hatred among citizens. And it is the intellectual force behind so much of the violence in our cities, suppression of free speech in our universities, and defamation of our treasured national statues and symbols.

To restore our society, academics must return to their vocation of relentlessly pursuing the truth and engaging in honest scholarship that seeks to understand the world and America's place in it.

The American Mind

Americans yearn for timeless stories and noble heroes that inspire them to be good, brave, diligent, daring, generous, honest, and compassionate.

Millions of Americans devour histories of the American Revolution and the Civil War and thrill to the tales of Washington, Jefferson, Hamilton, and Franklin, Lincoln and Grant, Sojourner Truth and Frederick Douglass. We still read the tales of Hawthorne and Melville, Twain and Poe, and the poems of Whitman and Dickinson. On Independence Day, we hum John Philip Sousa's "Stars and Stripes Forever" and sing along to Woody Guthrie's "This Land is Your Land." Americans applaud the loyalty, love, and kindness shared by the March sisters in *Little Women*, revere the rugged liberty of the cowboys in old westerns, and cheer the adventurous spirit of young Tom Sawyer. These great works have withstood the test of time because they speak to eternal truths and embody the American spirit.

It is up to America's artists, authors, filmmakers, musicians, social media influencers, and other culture leaders to carry on this tradition by once again giving shape and voice to America's self-understanding—to be what Jefferson called "an expression of the American mind."[3]

To them falls the creative task of writing stories, songs, and scripts that help to restore every American's conviction to embrace the good, lead virtuous lives, and act with an attitude of hope toward a better and bolder future for themselves, their families, and the entire nation.

Reverence for the Laws

The principles of equality and consent mean that all are equal before the law. No one is above the law, and no one is privileged to ignore the law, just as no one is outside the law in terms of its protection.

In his Lyceum Address, a young Abraham Lincoln warned of two results of a growing disregard for the rule of law. The first is mob rule: "whenever the vicious portion of [our] population shall be permitted to gather in bands of hundreds and thousands, and burn churches, ravage and rob provision stores, throw printing-presses into rivers, shoot editors, and hang and burn obnoxious persons at pleasure and with impunity, depend upon it, this government cannot last."

But Lincoln also warned of those of great ambition who thirst for distinction and, although "he would as willingly, perhaps more so, acquire it by doing good as harm, yet, that opportunity being past, and nothing left to be done in the way of building up, he would set boldly to the task of pulling down."

Statue of Abraham Lincoln by Daniel Chester French at the
Lincoln Memorial, Washington, D.C.
Source: Wikimedia Commons

Whether of the Left or of the Right, both mob rule and ty-
rannical rule violate the rule of law because both are rule by the
base passions rather than the better angels of our nature. Both
equally threaten our constitutional order.

When crimes go unpunished or when good men do nothing,
the lawless in spirit will become lawless in practice, leading to
violence and demagoguery.

Patriotic education must have at its center a respect for the rule of
law, including the Declaration and the Constitution, so that we have
what John Adams called "a government of laws, and not of men."[4]

In the end, Lincoln's solution must be ours:

Let every American, every lover of liberty, every well-wisher to
his posterity, swear by the blood of the Revolution, never to vio-

late in the least particular, the laws of the country; and never to tolerate their violation by others. As the patriots of seventy-six did to the support of the Declaration of Independence, so to the support of the Constitution and Laws, let every American pledge his life, his property, and his sacred honor;—let every man remember that to violate the law, is to trample on the blood of his father, and to tear the character of his own, and his children's liberty. Let reverence for the laws, be breathed by every American mother, to the lisping babe, that prattles on her lap—let it be taught in schools, in seminaries, and in colleges; let it be written in Primers, spelling books, and in Almanacs;—let it be preached from the pulpit, proclaimed in legislative halls, and enforced in courts of justice.[5]

VI

CONCLUSION

O N THE 150th Anniversary of the signing of the Declaration of Independence, President Calvin Coolidge raised the immortal banner in his time. "It is often asserted," he said, "that the world has made a great deal of progress since 1776 ... and that we may therefore very well discard their conclusions for something more modern. But that reasoning cannot be applied to this great charter. If all men are created equal, that is final. If they are endowed with inalienable rights, that is final. If governments derive their just powers from the consent of the governed, that is final. No advance, no progress can be made beyond these propositions."[1]

America's founding principles are true not because any generation—including our own—has lived them perfectly, but because they are based upon the eternal truths of the human condition. They are rooted in our capacity for evil and power for good, our longing for truth and striving for justice, our need for order and our love of freedom. Above all else, these principles recognize the worth, equality, potential, dignity, and glory of each and every man, woman, and child created in the image of God.

Throughout our history, our heroes—men and women, young and old, black and white, of many faiths and from all parts of the world—have changed America for the better not by abandoning these truths, but by appealing to them. Upon these universal ideals, they built a great nation, unified a strong people, and formed a beautiful way of life worth defending.

★ ★ ★

"The Declaration of Independence is the ring-bolt to the chain of your nation's destiny; so, indeed, I regard it. The principles contained in that instrument are saving principles. Stand by those principles, be true to them on all occasions, in all places, against all foes, and at whatever cost."

—Frederick Douglass

★ ★ ★

To be an American means something noble and good. It means treasuring freedom and embracing the vitality of self-government. We are shaped by the beauty, bounty, and wildness of our continent. We are united by the glory of our history. And we are distinguished by the American virtues of openness, honesty, optimism, determination, generosity, confidence, kindness, hard work, courage, and hope. Our principles did not create these virtues, but they laid the groundwork for them to grow and spread and forge America into the most just and glorious country in all of human history.

As we approach the 250th anniversary of our independence, we must resolve to teach future generations of Americans an accurate history of our country so that we all learn and cherish our founding principles once again. We must renew the pride and gratitude we have for this incredible nation that we are blessed to call home.

When we appreciate America for what she truly is, we know that our Declaration is worth preserving, our Constitution worth defending, our fellow citizens worth loving, and our country worth fighting for.

It is our task now to renew this commitment. So we proclaim, in the words our forefathers used two and a half centuries ago, "for the support of this Declaration, with a firm reliance on the protection of divine Providence, we mutually pledge to each other our Lives, our Fortunes, and our sacred Honor."

APPENDIX I

THE DECLARATION
OF INDEPENDENCE

IN CONGRESS, JULY 4, 1776

THE UNANIMOUS Declaration of the thirteen united States of America,

When in the Course of human events, it becomes necessary for one people to dissolve the political bands which have connected them with another, and to assume among the powers of the earth, the separate and equal station to which the Laws of Nature and of Nature's God entitle them, a decent respect to the opinions of mankind requires that they should declare the causes which impel them to the separation.

We hold these truths to be self-evident, that all men are created equal, that they are endowed by their Creator with certain unalienable Rights, that among these are Life, Liberty and the pursuit of Happiness. —That to secure these rights, Governments are instituted among Men, deriving their just powers from the consent of the governed, —That whenever any Form of Government becomes destructive of these ends, it is the Right of the People to alter or to abolish it, and to institute new Government, laying its foundation on such principles and organizing its powers in such form, as to them shall seem most likely to effect their Safety and Happiness. Prudence, indeed, will dictate that Governments long established should not be changed for light and transient causes; and accordingly all experience hath shewn, that mankind are more disposed to suffer, while evils are sufferable, than to right themselves by abolishing the forms to which they are accustomed. But when a long train of abuses and usurpations, pursuing invariably the same Object evinces a design to reduce them under absolute Despotism, it is their right, it is their duty, to throw off such Government, and to provide new Guards for their future security. —Such has been the patient sufferance of these Colonies; and such is now the necessity which constrains them to alter their former Systems of Government. The history of the present King of Great Britain is a history of repeated injuries and usurpations, all having in direct object the establishment of an absolute Tyranny over these States. To prove this, let Facts be submitted to a candid world.

He has refused his Assent to Laws, the most wholesome and necessary for the public good.

He has forbidden his Governors to pass Laws of immediate and pressing importance, unless suspended in their operation till his Assent should be obtained; and when so suspended, he has utterly neglected to attend to them.

He has refused to pass other Laws for the accommodation of large districts of people, unless those people would relinquish the right of Representation in the Legislature, a right inestimable to them and formidable to tyrants only.

He has called together legislative bodies at places unusual, uncomfortable, and distant from the depository of their public Records, for the sole purpose of fatiguing them into compliance with his measures.

He has dissolved Representative Houses repeatedly, for opposing with manly firmness his invasions on the rights of the people.

He has refused for a long time, after such dissolutions, to cause others to be elected; whereby the Legislative powers, incapable of Annihilation, have returned to the People at large for their exercise; the State remaining in the meantime exposed to all the dangers of invasion from without, and convulsions within.

He has endeavored to prevent the population of these States; for that purpose obstructing the Laws for Naturalization of Foreigners; refusing to pass others to encourage their migrations hither, and raising the conditions of new Appropriations of Lands.

He has obstructed the Administration of Justice, by refusing his Assent to Laws for establishing Judiciary powers.

He has made Judges dependent on his Will alone, for the tenure of their offices, and the amount and payment of their salaries.

He has erected a multitude of New Offices, and sent hither swarms of Officers to harass our people, and eat out their substance.

He has kept among us, in times of peace, Standing Armies without the Consent of our legislatures.

He has affected to render the Military independent of and superior to the Civil power.

He has combined with others to subject us to a jurisdiction foreign to our constitution, and unacknowledged by our laws; giving his Assent to their Acts of pretended Legislation:

For Quartering large bodies of armed troops among us:

For protecting them, by a mock Trial, from punishment for any Murders which they should commit on the Inhabitants of these States:

For cutting off our Trade with all parts of the world:

For imposing Taxes on us without our Consent:

For depriving us in many cases, of the benefits of Trial by Jury:

For transporting us beyond Seas to be tried for pretended offences

For abolishing the free System of English Laws in a neighboring Province, establishing therein an Arbitrary government, and enlarging its Boundaries so as to render it at once an example and fit instrument for introducing the same absolute rule into these Colonies:

For taking away our Charters, abolishing our most valuable Laws, and altering fundamentally the Forms of our Governments:

For suspending our own Legislatures, and declaring themselves invested with power to legislate for us in all cases whatsoever.

He has abdicated Government here, by declaring us out of his Protection and waging War against us.

He has plundered our seas, ravaged our Coasts, burnt our towns, and destroyed the lives of our people.

He is at this time transporting large Armies of foreign Mercenaries to complete the works of death, desolation and tyranny, already begun with circumstances of Cruelty & perfidy scarcely paralleled in the most barbarous ages, and totally unworthy the Head of a civilized nation.

He has constrained our fellow Citizens taken Captive on the high Seas to bear Arms against their Country, to become the executioners of their friends and Brethren, or to fall themselves by their Hands.

He has excited domestic insurrections amongst us, and has endeavored to bring on the inhabitants of our frontiers, the merciless Indian Savages, whose known rule of warfare, is an undistinguished destruction of all ages, sexes and conditions.

In every stage of these Oppressions We have Petitioned for Redress in the most humble terms: Our repeated Petitions have been answered only by repeated injury. A Prince whose character is thus marked by every act which may define a Tyrant, is unfit to be the ruler of a free people.

Nor have We been wanting in attentions to our British brethren. We have warned them from time to time of attempts by their legislature to extend an unwarrantable jurisdiction over us. We have reminded them of the circumstances of our emigration and settlement here. We have appealed to their native justice and magnanimity, and we have conjured them by the ties of our common kindred to disavow these usurpations, which, would inevitably interrupt our connections and correspondence. They too have been deaf to the voice of justice and of consanguinity. We must, therefore, acquiesce in the necessity, which denounces our Separation, and hold them, as we hold the rest of mankind, Enemies in War, in Peace Friends.

We, therefore, the Representatives of the united States of America, in General Congress, Assembled, appealing to the Supreme Judge of the world for the rectitude of our intentions, do, in the Name, and by Authority of the good People of these Colonies, solemnly publish and declare, That these United Colonies are, and of Right ought to be Free and Independent States; that they are Absolved from all Allegiance to the British Crown, and that all political connection between them and the State of Great Britain, is and ought to be totally dissolved; and that as Free and Independent States, they have full Power to levy War, conclude Peace, contract Alliances, establish Commerce, and to do all other Acts and Things which Independent States may of right do. And for the support of this Declaration, with a firm reliance on the protection of divine Providence, we mutually pledge to each other our Lives, our Fortunes and our sacred Honor.

APPENDIX II

FAITH AND
AMERICA'S PRINCIPLES

HISTORY UNDERSCORES the overwhelming importance of religious faith in American life, but some today see religious practice and political liberty to be in conflict and hold that religion is divisive and should be kept out of the public square. The founders of America held a very different view. They not only believed that all people have a right to religious liberty but also that religious faith is indispensable to the success of republican government. "The God who gave us life, gave us liberty at the same time," Thomas Jefferson once wrote. "The hand of force may destroy, but cannot disjoin them."[1]

The idea that faith sustains the principles of equality and natural rights is deeply rooted in American society and proven through human experience. The social, political, and personal value of religious faith within America's public space has been recognized and honored from the start. "Of all the dispositions and habits which lead to political prosperity, Religion and morality are indispensable supports," George Washington observed in his Farewell Address. "In vain would that man claim the tribute of Patriotism, who should labor to subvert these great Pillars of human happiness, these firmest props of the duties of Men and citizens." He went on to warn:

Let us with caution indulge the supposition, that morality can be maintained without religion. Whatever may be conceded to the influence of refined education on minds of peculiar structure, reason and experience both forbid us to expect that National morality can prevail in exclusion of religious principle.[2]

Civil and Religious Liberty

By the time of the American founding, political life in the West had undergone two momentous changes. The first was the sundering of civil from religious law. Prior to the widespread adoption of Christianity, Western societies made no distinction between civil and religious law, between the demands of the state and the demands of the gods. Laws against murder and theft, for instance, had the same status as laws compelling religious observance, and all laws were enforced by the same political institutions. Pagan societies recognized no "private sphere" of conscience into which the state may not justly intrude.

Christianity overturned this unity by separating political from religious obligation and making the latter primarily a matter of faith, superintended by a church whose authority was extrinsic to civil law. Thus began a millennium of tension and conflict between secular and ecclesiastical authorities.[3]

The second momentous change was the emergence of multiple sects within Christianity. In the pre-Christian world, all subjects or citizens of any given political community were expected to believe in and worship the same God or gods by the same rites and ceremonies. This basic unity held through the first several centuries of Christianity. But the Great Schism and, more significantly, the Reformation, undid Christian unity, which in turn greatly undermined political unity. Religious differences became sources of political conflict and war. The nations of Europe fell into internal sectarian divisions and external religious-political wars.

British monarchs not only disputed one another's claims to the throne but imposed their preferred religious doctrines on the whole nation. Gruesome tortures and political imprisonments were common. The Puritans proclaimed a "commonwealth" which executed the Anglican king. The executed king's son proceeded to supplant the "commonwealth," but because his brother was suspected of being Catholic, Protestants expelled him in the so-called "Glorious Revolution" of 1688 that installed the Protestant monarch of the Netherlands and his wife as England's king and queen.

In the 17th century, religious believers of many stripes came to North America as refugees from Europe's religious persecutions. Ironically, the most famous attempt to form a separate religious community—the Pilgrims' relocation to Massachusetts—eventually led to the core American principle of religious liberty.

The Founders' Solution

The founders were ever mindful of the religious oppression and persecution that had existed throughout history. They knew that religious zeal often leads to the assumption that specific beliefs should be "established" by governments, meaning certain religious doctrines should be enforced by law as the official religion of the state. Individuals who are not members of that religious body and do not accept its teachings often did not enjoy the same rights as a result. Discriminations against nonbelievers ranged from mild to the most awful, but the "establishment" of one religious body by government always divided the population into privileged and non-privileged classes, resulting in endless bitter struggles for religious dominance.

At the same time, the founders recognized man's natural yearning to pursue the truth about God and freely practice the teachings inspired by those religious beliefs. They knew that religious beliefs, good for the ultimate happiness of the individual, were also good for politics because they encouraged the virtues (such as justice, self-restraint, courage, and truthfulness) necessary for self-government. To violate the consciences of citizens by using force to change their religious beliefs was a gross injustice. Violations of conscience by government would not strengthen the attachment of citizens to their government but would only foster hypocrisy, hatred, and rebellion.

The American founders did not claim to settle the ultimate questions of reason and revelation. But for the first time in history, the founders believed they saw a *practicable* and just alternative to religious persecution and conflict. Unlike previous forms of government, the Constitution they framed did not include the power to "establish" a national religion, and it specifically denied that anyone could be prevented from holding office by a "religious test." They underlined this by *expressly* forbidding the federal government in the First Amendment from "establishing" any religion and, to make it even clearer, guaranteeing the free exercise of religion.

Together, these provisions give religious liberty primacy among the natural rights secured by our Constitution. This follows from the principles of the Declaration, as the foremost way individuals fulfill their well-being—in exercising their natural right to "the pursuit of happiness"—is through the religious teachings and institutions they believe and hope will lead to their salvation.

We often use the phrase "the separation of church and state" to refer to the founders' practical settlement of these questions, but this phrase is usually misunderstood to mean a complete separation of religion and politics, which is a very different idea.[4] When the founders denied government the power to establish a religion, they did not intend to expunge religion from political life but to make room for the religious beliefs and free expression of all citizens.

The Common Ground of Reason and Revelation

The founders emphasized where the moral teachings of religious faith and the ground of political liberty were in agreement. Just as they were confident that government has no theological expertise to decide the path to salvation, they were equally confident that a well-designed republican constitution is sanctioned by human nature and open to moral reasoning shared among human beings.

General moral precepts can be understood by human reason, and faith echoes these precepts. In other words, when the Declaration of Independence opens by appealing to "the Laws of Nature and of Nature's God," it means that there is a human morality accessible to both reason and revelation. This is the common moral ground of the American founding, where reason and revelation work together for civil and religious liberty. Consider this from the Reverend Samuel Cooper in 1780:

We want not, indeed, a special revelation from heaven to teach us that men are born equal and free; that no man has a natural claim of dominion over his neighbors. . . . These are the plain dictates of that reason and common sense with which the common parent of men has informed the human bosom. It is, however, a satisfaction to observe such everlasting maxims of equity confirmed, and impressed upon the consciences of men, by the instructions, precepts, and examples given us in the sacred oracles; one internal mark of their divine original, and that they come from him "who hath made of one blood all nations to dwell upon the face of the earth." [Acts 17:26][5]

In proclaiming the self-evident truths of the Declaration, the founders interwove reason and revelation into America's creed. One such truth is that there are fixed laws higher than those enacted by governments. Reason and faith secure limits on the reach of man-made laws, thereby opening up the space for civil and religious liberty. Another is that, in the act of creation, however conceived, all came into existence as equals: the Creator gives no person or group a higher right to rule others without their agreement. Yet another is that all are gifted through their human nature with intrinsic rights which they cannot sign away, above all the great rights of "Life, Liberty, and the Pursuit of Happiness." In all of these things, *the founders limited the ends of government in order to open up the higher ends of man.*

The purpose of the founders' ingenious division of church and state was neither to weaken the importance of faith nor to set up a secular state, but to open up the public space of society to a common American morality.* Religious institutions, which were influential before the American Revolution, became powerful witnesses for the advancement of equality, freedom, opportunity, and human dignity.

- The American Revolution might not have taken place or succeeded without the moral ideas spread through the pulpits, sermons, and publications of Christian instructors. On the nation's 150th Independence Day celebration,

---

* "Enlightened by a benign religion, professed, indeed, and practiced in various forms, yet all of them inculcating honesty, truth, temperance, gratitude, and the love of man; acknowledging and adoring an overruling Providence, which by all its dispensations proves that it delights in the happiness of man here and his greater happiness hereafter—with all these blessings, what more is necessary to make us a happy and a prosperous people?" Thomas Jefferson, "First Inaugural Address," in Writings, ed. Merrill D. Peterson (New York, NY: The Library of America, 2011), 494. By 1835, Alexis de Tocqueville could make the following observation: "Religion, which, among Americans, never mixes directly in the government of society, should therefore be considered as the first of their political institutions; for if it does not give them the taste for freedom, it singularly facilitates their use of it.... I do not know if all Americans have faith in their religion—for who can read to the bottom of hearts?—but I am sure that they believe it necessary to the maintenance of republican institutions. This opinion does not belong only to one class of citizens or to one party, but to the entire nation; one finds it in all ranks." Alexis de Tocqueville, *Democracy in America*, ed. Harvey C. Mansfield and Delba Winthrop (Chicago: University of Chicago Press, 2000), 280.

President Calvin Coolidge said that the principles of the Declaration of Independence were

> found in the text, the sermons and the writings of the early colonial clergy who were earnestly undertaking to instruct their congregations in the great mystery of how to live. They preached equality because they believed in the fatherhood of God and the brotherhood of man. They justified freedom by the text that we are all created in the divine image, all partakers of the divine spirit.[6]

- Even before the eighteenth century, Quakers and the faithful of other denominations, drawing on the Bible and on philosophy, began a crusade to abolish race-based slavery in the colonies. Anti-slavery literature was largely faith-based and spread through the free states via churches. One of the most famous anti-slavery writers in history, Harriet Beecher Stowe, was the devout daughter of a great American reformist clergyman and wife of a well-known theologian. Her worldwide best-seller, *Uncle Tom's Cabin*, fired the moral indignation of millions that helped lay the ground for abolition.[7]

- America's greatest reform movements have been founded or promoted by religious leaders and laypersons reared in faithful home environments. Mother Elizabeth Ann Seton in the early nineteenth century set up orphanages and established free schools for poor girls. The tireless effort to end Jim Crow and extend civil and voting rights to African Americans and other minorities was driven by clergy and lay faithful of a multitude of denominations, including most prominently the Reverend Martin Luther King, Jr., who used nonviolent tactics to advocate for equal rights. The Pro-Life Movement today is led by clergy and the faithful of virtually every denomination.

- Local religious leaders have been a key buttress supporting our communities. Neighborhood and parish churches, temples, and mosques still are the strongest organized centers of help for the local poor, jobless, homeless, and families down on their luck. For generations, neighbors have assisted neighbors through church networks, helping the needy avoid the dehumanization of prolonged dependency on government welfare. Today, countless men and women actively feed and care for the poor, house and speak for immigrants and the disadvantaged, minister to jailed and released criminals, and advocate powerfully for a better society and a more peaceful world, supported by the charitable funding of Americans of all faiths.

- Clergy of various denominations have sacrificed career goals and risked their lives in order to minister to men and women serving in the armed forces. The brave soldiers who protect America against foreign dangers depend on the corps of military chaplains who help cultivate the warriors' courage, inner strength, and perseverance they need to succeed in their missions. Religious chaplains open every session of Congress, and clergy pray at presidential inaugurals, state funerals, and other official occasions.

Conclusion

The United States has journeyed far since its founding. While the founders certainly had disagreements about the nature of religion, they had little doubt that faith was essential to the new experiment in self-government and republican constitutionalism. They knew that citizens who practiced the faith under the protection of religious liberty would support the Constitution that embodies their rights.

The shared morality of faithful citizens would sustain a republican culture that would foster stable family relationships and encourage important virtues like fortitude to defend the nation in war, self-restraint over physical appetites or lust for wealth, compassion toward neighbors and strangers in need, self-disciplined labor, intellectual integrity, independence from long-term reliance on private or public benefits, justice in all relationships, prudence in judging the common good, courage to defend their rights and liberties, and finally, piety towards the Creator whose favor determines the well-being of society.

We have arrived at a point where the most influential part of our nation finds these old faith-based virtues dangerous, useless, or perhaps even laughable. At the same time, many Americans feel that we have veered off the path that has brought so many happiness and success, and fear a growing factionalism cannot be overcome merely by electing a different president or political party. How can America overcome this partisan divide?

The answer to this rising concern must begin by frankly and humbly admitting that the common ground of equal natural rights on which our common morality is based is no longer visible to many Americans.* We must refocus on the proposition that united this nation from the beginning: the proposition of the Declaration of Independence that there are "self-evident truths" which unite all Americans under a common creed.

But it is almost impossible to hold to this creed—which describes what and who we *are*—without reference to the Creator as the ultimate source of human equality and natural rights. This is the deepest reason why the founders saw faith as the key to good character as well as good citizenship, and why we must remain "one Nation under God, indivisible, with liberty and justice for all."

The proposition of political equality is powerfully supported by biblical faith, which confirms that all human beings are equal in dignity and created in God's image. Every form of religious faith is entitled to religious liberty, so long as all comprehend and sincerely assent to the fundamental principle that under

---

* Consider this from a Yale Law School professor: "The potential transformation of the Establishment Clause from a guardian of religious liberty into a guarantor of public secularism raises prospects at once dismal and dreadful. The more that the clause is used to disable religious groups from active involvement in the programs of the welfare state, or, for that matter, from active involvement in the public square that is the crucible of public policy, the less the religions will be able to play their proper democratic role of mediating between the individual and the state and the less they will be able to play their proper theological role of protecting the people of God. . . . Maybe it is just another effort to ensure that intermediate institutions, such as the religions, do not get in the way of the government's will. Perhaps, in short, it is a way of ensuring that only one vision of the meaning of reality—that of the powerful group of individuals called the state—is allowed a political role. Back in Tocqueville's day, this was called tyranny. Nowadays, all too often, but quite mistakenly, it is called the separation of church and state." Stephen L. Carter, *The Culture of Disbelief: How American Law and Politics Trivialize Religious Devotion* (New York: Basic Books, 1993), 122-3.

"the Laws of Nature and of Nature's God" all human beings are equally endowed with unalienable rights to life, liberty, and the pursuit of happiness. As the first American president wrote in 1790 to the Hebrew Congregation in Newport, Rhode Island:

> The Citizens of the United States of America have a right to applaud themselves for having given to mankind examples of an enlarged and liberal policy: a policy worthy of imitation. All possess alike liberty of conscience and immunities of citizenship. It is now no more that toleration is spoken of, as if it was by the indulgence of one class of people, that another enjoyed the exercise of their inherent natural rights. For happily the Government of the United States, which gives to bigotry no sanction, to persecution no assistance, requires only that they who live under its protection should demean themselves as good citizens, in giving it on all occasions their effectual support.[8]

APPENDIX III

CREATED EQUAL OR IDENTITY POLITICS?

A MERICANS ARE deeply committed to the principle of equality enshrined in the Declaration of Independence, that all are created equal and equally endowed with natural rights to life, liberty, and the pursuit of happiness. This creed, as Abraham Lincoln once noted, is "the electric cord" that "links the hearts of patriotic and liberty-loving" people everywhere, no matter their race or country of origin.[1] The task of American civic education is to transmit this creed from one generation of Americans to the next.

In recent times, however, a new creed has arisen challenging the original one enshrined in the Declaration of Independence. This new creed, loosely defined as identity politics, has three key features. First, the creed of identity politics defines and divides Americans in terms of collective social identities. According to this new creed, our racial and sexual identities are more important than our common status as individuals equally endowed with fundamental rights.

Second, the creed of identity politics ranks these different racial and social groups in terms of privilege and power, with disproportionate moral worth allotted to each. It divides Americans into two groups: oppressors and victims. The more a group is considered oppressed, the more its members have a moral claim upon the rest of society. As for their supposed oppressors, they must atone and even be punished in perpetuity for their sins and those of their ancestors.

Third, the creed of identity politics teaches that America itself is to blame for oppression. America's "electric cord" is not the creed of liberty and equality that connects citizens today to each other and to every generation of Americans past, present, and future. Rather, America's "electric cord" is a heritage of oppression that the majority racial group inflicts upon minority groups, and identity politics is about assigning and absolving guilt for that oppression.

According to this new creed, Americans are not a people defined by their dedication to human equality, but a people defined by their perpetuation of racial and sexual oppression.

The Historical Precedent for Identity Politics

Whereas the Declaration of Independence founded a nation grounded on human equality and equal rights, identity politics sees a nation defined by oppressive hierarchies. But this vision of America is actually not new. While identity politics may seem novel and ground-breaking, it resurrects prior attempts in American history to deny the meaning of equality enshrined in the Declaration. In portraying America as racist and white supremacist, identity politics advocates follow Lincoln's great rival Stephen A. Douglas, who wrongly claimed that American government "was made on the white basis" "by white men, for the benefit of white men."* Indeed, there are uncanny similarities between 21st century activists of identity politics and 19th century apologists for slavery.

John C. Calhoun is perhaps the leading forerunner of identity politics. Rejecting America's common political identity that follows from the Declaration's principles, he argued that the American polity was not an actual community at all but was reducible only to diverse majority and minority groups. Calhoun saw these groups as more or less permanent, slowly evolving products of their race and particular historical circumstances.

Like modern-day proponents of identity politics, Calhoun believed that achieving unity through rational deliberation and political compromise was impossible; majority groups would only use the political process to oppress minority groups. In Calhoun's America, respect for each group demanded that each hold a veto over the actions of the wider community. But Calhoun also argued that some groups must outrank others in the majoritarian

---

* Douglas' unsubstantiated claim, also made by Chief Justice Taney and echoed today in many textbooks, was that the founders did not include blacks in the Declaration of Independence. Stephen Douglas, "Third Debate with Lincoln at Jonesboro, Illinois" in *The Collected Works of Abraham Lincoln*, ed. Roy P. Basler, vol. 3 (New Brunswick: Rutgers University Press, 1990), 112. Lincoln responded in the Fifth Debate at Galesburg, Illinois: "The entire records of the world, from the date of the Declaration of Independence up to within three years ago, may be searched in vain for one single affirmation, from one single man, that the negro was not included in the Declaration of Independence; I think I may defy Judge Douglas to show that he ever said so, that Washington ever said so, that any President ever said so, that any member of Congress ever said so, or that any living man upon the whole earth ever said so." Abraham Lincoln, "Fifth Debate with Stephen A. Douglas at Galesburg, Illinois," in *The Collected Works of Abraham Lincoln*, ed. Roy P. Basler, vol. 3 (New Brunswick, NJ: Rutgers Univ. Press, 1990), 220.

decision-making process. In Calhoun's America, one minority group—Southern slaveholders—could veto any attempt by the majority group—Northern States—to restrict or abolish the enslavement of another group. In the context of American history, *the original form of identity politics was used to defend slavery.*†

As American history teaches, dividing citizens into identity groups, especially on the basis of race, is a recipe for stoking enmity among all citizens. It took the torrent of blood spilled in the Civil War and decades of subsequent struggles to expunge Calhoun's idea of group hierarchies from American public life. Nevertheless, activists pushing identity politics want to resuscitate a modified version of his ideas, rejecting the Declaration's principle of equality and defining Americans once again in terms of group hierarchies. They aim to make this the defining creed of American public life, and they have been working for decades to bring it about.

Intellectual Origins of Identity Politics

The modern revival of identity politics stems from mid-20th century European thinkers who sought the revolutionary over-

---

† "It is a great and dangerous error to suppose that all people are equally entitled to liberty. It is a reward to be earned, not a blessing to be gratuitously lavished on all alike—a reward reserved for the intelligent, the patriotic, the virtuous and deserving—and not a boon to be bestowed on a people too ignorant, degraded and vicious, to be capable either of appreciating or of enjoying it.... A reward more appropriate than liberty could not be conferred on the deserving—nor a punishment inflicted on the undeserving more just, than to be subject to lawless and despotic rule." John C. Calhoun, "A Disquisition on Government," in *Union and Liberty: The Political Philosophy of John C. Calhoun*, ed. Ross M. Lence (Indianapolis: Liberty Fund, 1992), 42. For analysis of Calhoun, see Harry V. Jaffa, *A New Birth of Freedom: Abraham Lincoln and the Coming of the Civil War* (Lanham: Rowman & Littlefield Publishers, 2000), 403-471.

throw of their political and social systems but were disillusioned by the working class's lack of interest in inciting revolution. This setback forced revolutionaries to reconsider their strategy.

One of the most prominent, the Italian Marxist Antonio Gramsci, argued that the focus should not be on economic revolution as much as taking control of the institutions that shape culture. In Gramsci's language, revolutionaries should focus on countering the "Hegemonic Narrative" of the established culture with a "Counter-Narrative," creating a counter-culture that subverts and seeks to destroy the established culture.[2]

Gramsci was an important influence on the thinkers of the "Frankfurt School" in Germany, who developed a set of revolutionary ideas called Critical Theory. Herbert Marcuse, one member of the Frankfurt School who immigrated to the United States in the 1940s, became the intellectual godfather of American identity politics. With little hope that the white American worker could be coaxed to revolution, Marcuse focused not on instigating class conflict but on instigating cultural conflicts around racial identity. He saw revolutionary potential in "the substratum of the outcasts and outsiders, the exploited and persecuted of other races and other colors."[3]

These ideas led to the development of Critical Race Theory, a variation of critical theory applied to the American context that stresses racial divisions and sees society in terms of minority racial groups oppressed by the white majority.[4] Equally significant to its intellectual content is the role Critical Race Theory plays in promoting fundamental social transformation. Following Gramsci's strategy of taking control of the culture, Marcuse's followers use the approach of Critical Race Theory to impart an oppressor-victim narrative upon generations of Americans. This work of cultural revolution has been going on for decades, and its first political reverberations can be seen in 1960s America.

The Radicalization of American Politics in the 1960s

Prior to the 1960s, movements in American history that sought to end racial and sexual discrimination, such as abolition, women's suffrage, or the Civil Rights Movement, did so on the ground set by the Declaration of Independence.

In leading the Civil Rights Movement, Martin Luther King, Jr., was aware that other, more revolutionary groups wanted to fight in terms of group identities. In his "I Have a Dream" speech, King rejected hateful stereotyping based on a racialized group identity. The "marvelous new militancy which has engulfed the Negro community must not lead us to distrust all white people," he warned. King refused to define Americans in terms of permanent racialized identities and called on Americans "to lift our nation from the quicksands of racial injustice to the solid rock of brotherhood" and see ourselves as one nation united by a common political creed and commitment to Christian love.

"When the architects of our republic wrote the magnificent words of the Constitution and the Declaration of Independence, they were signing a promissory note to which every American was to fall heir," King wrote. "This note was a promise that all men, yes, black men as well as white men, would be guaranteed the unalienable rights to life, liberty, and the pursuit of happiness."[5]

As the 1960s advanced, however, many rejected King's formulation of civil rights and reframed debates about equality in terms of racial and sexual identities. The Civil Rights Movement came to abandon the nondiscrimination and equal opportunity of colorblind civil rights in favor of "group rights" and preferential treatment.* A radical women's liberation movement reimagined America as a patriarchal system, asserting that every woman is a victim of oppression by men. The Black Power and black nationalist movements reimagined America as a white supremacist regime. Meanwhile, other activists constructed artificial groupings to further divide Americans by race, creating new categories like "Asian American" and "Hispanic" to teach Americans to think of themselves in terms of group identities and to rouse various groups into politically cohesive bodies.[6]

The Incompatibility of Identity Politics with American Principles

Identity politics divide Americans by placing them perpetually in conflict with each other. This extreme ideology assaults and undermines the American principle of equality in several key ways.

* The Civil Rights Act of 1964 was a fulfilment of the Reconstruction Amendments to the Constitution, which in turn reflected the acknowledgement that the Declaration of Independence is the foundation of the Constitution. But this pivotal law based on protecting individual rights was reinterpreted by the bureaucracy and subsequently by the courts to define Americans by group identities. Thus came about racial quotas in employment discrimination cases, busing in school segregation cases, and, subsequently, racial redistricting in voting rights cases. This transformation is described in detail in Hugh Davis Graham, *The Civil Rights Era: Origin and Development of National Policy, 1960-1972* (New York: Oxford University Press, 1990). An abridged version is *Civil Rights and the Presidency: Race and Gender in American Politics, 1960-1972*. The administrative state's development of race conscious policies is related by Herman Belz, *Equality Transformed: A Quarter-Century of Affirmative Action* (New Brunswick: Transaction, 1991). Paul Moreno studies the New Deal background of civil rights policy in *From Direct Action to Affirmative Action: Fair Employment Law and Policy in America, 1933-1972* (Baton Rouge: Louisiana State University Press, 1997).

First, identity politics attacks American self-government. Through the separation of powers and the system of checks and balances, American constitutionalism prevents any one group from having complete control of the government. In order to form a majority, the various groups that comprise the nation must resolve their disagreements in light of shared principles and come to a deliberative consensus over how best to govern. In the American system, public policy is decided by prudential compromise among different interest groups for the sake of the common good.

Identity politics, on the other hand, sees politics as the realm of permanent conflict and struggle among racial, gender, and other groups, and no compromise between different groups is possible. Rational deliberation and compromise only preserve the oppressive status quo.[7] Instead, identity politics relies on humiliation, intimidation, and coercion. American self-government, where all citizens are equal before the law, is supplanted by a system where certain people use their group identity to get what they want.

Second, by dividing Americans into oppressed and oppressor groups, activists of identity politics propose to punish some citizens—many times for wrongs their ancestors allegedly committed—while rewarding others. Members of oppressed groups must ascend, and members of oppressor groups must descend. This new system denies that human beings are endowed with the same rights, and creates new hierarchies with destructive assumptions and practices.

On the one hand, members of oppressed groups are told to abandon their shared civic identity as Americans and think of themselves in terms of their sexual or racial status. The consequence is that they should no longer see themselves as agents responsible for their own actions but as victims controlled by impersonal forces. In a word, they must reject, not affirm, the Declaration's understanding of self-government according to the consent of the governed. If members of oppressed groups want to become free, they must rely upon a regime of rewards and privileges assigned according to group identity.

On the other hand, members of oppressor groups merit public humiliation at the hands of others. Diversity training programs, for example, force members of "oppressor" groups to confess before their co-workers how they contribute to racism. Educational programs based on identity politics often use a person's race to degrade or ostracize them.

These degradations of individuals on the basis of race expose the lie that identity politics promotes the equal protection of rights. Advocates of identity politics argue that all hate speech should be banned but then define hate speech as only applying to protected identity groups who are in turn free to say whatever they want about their purported oppressors. This leads to a "cancel culture" that punishes those who violate the terms of identity politics.

Third, identity politics denies the fundamental moral tenet of the Declaration, that human beings are equal by nature. This founding principle provides a permanent and immutable standard for remedying wrongs done to Americans on the basis of race, sex, or any group identity.

Repudiating this universal tenet, activists pushing identity politics rely instead on cultural and historical generalizations about which groups have stronger moral claims than others. They claim this approach offers a superior and more historically sensitive moral standard. But unlike the standard based on a common humanity—what Lincoln called "an abstract truth, applicable to all men and all times"[8]—their historical standard is not permanent. Rather, it adjusts to meet the political fashions of a particular moment. By this standard, ethnicities that were once considered "oppressed" can in short order turn into "oppressors," and a standard that can turn a minority from victim to villain within the course of a few years is no standard at all.

Fourth, identity-politics activists often are radicals whose political program is fundamentally incompatible not only with the principles of the Declaration of Independence but also the rule of law embodied by the United States Constitution. Antagonism to the creed expressed in the Declaration seems not an option but a necessary part of their strategy. When activists are discussing seemingly innocuous campaigns to promote "diversity," they are often aiming for fundamental structural change.

Conclusion

Identity politics is fundamentally incompatible with the principle of equality enshrined in the Declaration of Independence.

Proponents of identity politics rearrange Americans by group identities, rank them by how much oppression they have experienced at the hands of the majority culture, and then sow division among them. While not as barbaric or dehumanizing, this new creed creates new hierarchies as unjust as the old hierarchies of the antebellum South, making a mockery of equality with an ever-changing scale of special privileges on the basis of racial and sexual identities. The very idea of equality under the law—of one nation sharing King's "solid rock of brotherhood"—is not possible and, according to this argument, probably not even desirable.

All Americans, and especially all educators, should understand identity politics for what it is: rejection of the principle of equality proclaimed in the Declaration of Independence. As a nation, we should oppose such efforts to divide us and reaffirm our common faith in the fundamental equal right of every individual to life, liberty, and the pursuit of happiness.

APPENDIX IV

TEACHING AMERICANS ABOUT THEIR COUNTRY

A MERICA'S FOUNDERS understood the importance of education to the long-term success or failure of the American experiment in self-government. Liberty and learning are intimately intertwined and rely on each other for protection and nurturing. As James Madison noted, "What spectacle can be more edifying or more seasonable, than that of Liberty and Learning, each leaning on the other for their mutual and surest support?"[1]

Education in civics, history, and literature holds the central place in the well-being of both students and communities. For republican government, citizens with such an education are essential. The knowledge of human nature and unalienable rights—understanding what it means to be human—brings a deeper perspective to public affairs, for the simple reason that educated citizens will take encouragement or warning from our past in order to navigate the present.

A wholesome education also passes on the stories of great Americans from the past who have contributed their genius, sacrifices, and lives to build and preserve this nation. They strengthen the bond that a vast and diverse people can point to as that which makes us one community, fostered by civil political conversation and a shared and grateful memory.

The crucial contribution that a quality civics education makes to the well-being of America and its citizens is love for our country, properly understood. A healthy attachment to this country—true patriotism—is neither blind to its flaws nor fanatical in believing that America is the source of all good. Rather, the right sort of love of country holds it up to an objective standard of right and wrong, with the desire and intent that the country do what is right. Where the country has done what is good, citizens justly praise those who came before them. Where it has done wrong, they should criticize the country and work to make sure that we—the people who govern it—do what is right.

Rather than cast aside the serious study of America's founding principles or breed contempt for America's heritage, our educational system should aim to teach students about the true principles and history of their country—a history that is "accurate, honest, unifying, inspiring, and ennobling."

The Misuse of History

To begin such an education, we must first avoid an all-too-common mistake. It is wrong to think of history by itself as the standard for judgment. The standard is set by unchanging principles that transcend history. Our founders called these "self-evident truths" and published these truths for all the world to see in the Declaration of Independence: there are "Laws of Nature and of Nature's God" that inform human interactions, all human beings are created equal, and all human beings have fundamental rights that are theirs as human beings, not the gift of government.

Consider the subject of slavery. At the time the Declaration was written, between fifteen and twenty percent of the American people were held as slaves. This brutal, humiliating fact so contradicted the principles of equality and liberty announced in 1776 that many people now make the mistake of denouncing equality and liberty. Yet as we condemn slavery now, we learn from the founders' public statements and private letters that they condemned it then. One great reason they published the Declaration's bold words was to show that slavery is a wrong according to nature and according to God. With this Declaration, they started the new nation on a path that would lead to the end of slavery. As Abraham Lincoln explained, the founding generation was in no position to end this monstrous crime in one stroke, but they did mean "to declare the right, so that the enforcement of it might follow as fast as circumstances should permit."[2]

The point is this: The key to freedom for all is discovered in the moral standard proclaimed in the Declaration. It would, the founders hoped, prove to be the key that would unlock the door to equality and liberty for all. *History* tells the story of how our country has succeeded—and at times failed—in living up to the standard of right and wrong. Our task as citizens in a national community is to live—and it is the task of teachers to teach—so as to keep our community in line with our *principles*.

The purpose of genuine, liberal education is to come to know what it means to be free. Education seeks knowledge of the nature of things, especially of human nature and of the universe as a whole. Man is that special part of the universe that seeks to know where we stand within it. We wonder about its origins. The human person is driven by a yearning for self-knowledge, seeking to understand the essential nature and purpose of his or her life and what it means to carry that life out in relationship with others.

The surest guides for this quest to understand freedom and human nature are the timeless works of philosophy, political thought, literature, history, oratory, and art that civilization has produced. Contrary to what is sometimes claimed, these works are not terribly difficult to identify: they are marked by their foundational and permanent character and their ability to transcend the time and landscape of their creation. No honest, intelligent surveyor of human civilization could deny the unique brilliance of Homer or Plato, Dante or Shakespeare, Washington or Lincoln, Melville or Hawthorne.

But far too little of this guidance is given in American classrooms today. In most K-12 social studies and civics classes, serious study of the principles of equality and liberty has vanished. The result has been a rising generation of young citizens who know little about the origins and stories of their country, and less about the true standards of equality and liberty. This trend is neither new nor unreported, but it is leaving a terrible and growing void as students suffer from both the ignorance of not realizing what they lack, and a certain arrogance that they have no need to find out.

The Decline of American Education

This pronounced decline of American education began in the late nineteenth century when progressive reformers began discarding the traditional understanding of education. The old understanding involved conveying a body of transcendent knowledge and practical wisdom that had been passed down for generations and which aimed to develop the character and intellect of the student. The new education, by contrast, pursued contradictory goals that are at the same time mundane and unrealistically utopian.

In the view of these progressive educators, human nature is ever-changing, so the task of the new education was to remake people in order to improve the human condition. They sought to reshape students in the image they thought best, and education became an effort to engineer the way students think.*

This new education deemed itself "pragmatic," subordinating America's students to the demands of the new industrial economy for skills-based, jobs-oriented training. Rather than examine the past for those unchanging truths and insights into our shared humanity, students today are taught to assume that the founders' views were narrow and deficient: *that's just how people used to think, but we know better now.*

Under this new approach, the only reason to study the works of

---

* "Liberalism is committed to the idea of historic relativity. It knows that the content of the individual and freedom change with time; that this is as true of social change as it is of individual development from infancy to maturity. The positive counterpart of opposition to doctrinal absolutism is experimentalism. The connection between historic relativity and experimental method is intrinsic. Time signifies change. The significance of individuality with respect to social policies alters with change of the conditions in which individuals live. The earlier liberalism [of the American Founders] in being absolute was also unhistoric." John Dewey, "The Future of Liberalism," in *The Later Works of John Dewey 1925-1953*, ed. Jo Ann Boydston (Southern Illinois University Press, 1987), 291-292. And on education proper: "I believe that education is a regulation of the process of coming to share in the social consciousness; and that the adjustment of individual activity on the basis of this social consciousness is the only sure method of social reconstruction." John Dewey, *My Pedagogic Creed* (New York: E. L. Kellogg & Co, 1897), 16.

Aristotle, Shakespeare, or America's founders is not to learn how to be virtuous, self-governing citizens, not to learn anything true, good, or beautiful, but to realize how such figures of yesteryear are unfit for the present day. Such a vision of education teaches that ideas evolve as human progress marches on, as supposedly old and worn ideas are cast aside on the so-called "wrong side of history."

This new education replaced humane and liberal education in many places, and alienated Americans from their own nature, their own identities, and their own place and time. It cuts students off from understanding that which came before them. Like square pegs and round holes, students are made to fit the latest expert theory about where history is headed next.

As the twentieth century continued, these progressive views reached their logical apex: there is no ultimate or objective truth, only various expressions of different cultures' beliefs. Wittingly or unwittingly, progressives concluded that truth is an ideological construct created by those with inordinate wealth and power to further their own particular agendas. In such a relativist environment, progressive education may as well impose its own ideological construct on the future. They did not call it indoctrination, but that is what it is.

Since the 1960s, an even more radicalized challenge has emerged. This newer challenge arrived under the feel-good names of "liberation" and "social justice." Instead of offering a comprehensive, unifying human story, these ideological approaches diminish our shared history and disunite the country by setting certain communities against others. History is no longer tragic but melodramatic, in which all that can be learned from studying the past is that groups victimize and oppress each other.

By turning to bitterness and judgment, distorted histories

of those like Howard Zinn or the journalists behind the "1619 Project" have prevented their students from learning to think inductively with a rich repository of cultural, historical, and literary referents. Such works do not respect their students' independence as young thinkers trying to grapple with social complexity while forming their empirical judgments about it. They disdain today's students, just as they doubt the humanity, goodness, or benevolence in America's greatest historical figures. They see only weaknesses and failures, teaching students truth is an illusion, that hypocrisy is everywhere, and that power is all that matters.

A few reforms of note have been attempted to improve America's civic educational system, but they fail to address the key problems.

The first was embraced with good intentions. Common Core appeared to be a promising way for the federal government to supply a framework to improve the nation's schools. But the Constitution leaves education to the states and localities and denies the federal government any authority to impose what it wants to be taught in the nation's schools.* To surmount this obstacle, the federal government used significant federal funding to entice states to adopt Common Core. Nevertheless, within a few years it became clear that students in states that "voluntarily" adopted Common Core suffered significantly lower academic performance

---

* In addition to lacking any authority under the Constitution, federal law prevents any officer or employee of the federal government from mandating, directing, or controlling a state, local educational agency, or school's specific instructional content, academic standards and assessments, curricula, or program of instruction. This law was amended in 2015 to prevent the federal government further from doing the same through grants, contracts, or other cooperative agreements. See *Every Student Succeeds Act*, Public Law 114-95, Section 8526A (2015).

and fewer marketable skills than comparable cohorts of students who had been educated outside the Common Core regime. This system of micromanaged "standards" proved to be a recipe for bureaucratic control and sterile conformity instead of a pathway towards better instruction. We learned from the failed Common Core experiment that one-size-fits-all national models are a blueprint for trivializing and mechanizing learning.[3]

A more recently proposed remedy is called the "New Civics" (or "Action Civics"). The progressive approach to education rests on the faulty notion that knowledge concerning long-term human and social concerns is divided between "facts" (scientific data separated from judgments about right and wrong) and "values" (preferences about moral matters, such as justice, which are said to have no objective status). Most students, yearning to make the world better, find the study of "facts" boring and meaningless. The New Civics approach is to prioritize a values-oriented praxis over fact-based knowledge. As a result, New Civics uses direct community service and political action (such as protesting for gun control or lobbying for laws to address climate change) to teach students to bring change to the system itself. Under this guise, civics education becomes less about teaching civic knowledge and more about encouraging contemporary policy positions.[4]

However well-intended, the New Civics only aggravates the already inherent problems of progressive education. Dispensing with ideas that transcend and inform history, students lack criteria for judging what a politically healthy nation looks like and they cannot defend what practical actions actually would improve the health of their community. A well-formulated education in political and moral principles is the necessary source of the knowledge citizens need to make wise judgments about voting, demonstrating, or any other civic activity. By neglecting true civic education, the New Civics movement only compounds the mistakes of today's conventional education in civics.

What is Authentic Education?

There are many aspects of formal education. The importance of professional education and technical training is not here in dispute. There is no question that one crucial purpose of education is to equip individuals with the knowledge and skills they need to provide for themselves and their families. More fundamental is the broader and deeper education called liberal education.*

Education liberates human beings in the true sense—liberation from ignorance and confusion, from prejudice and delusion, and from untamed passions and fanciful hopes that degrade and

---

* Since antiquity, the liberal arts have occupied a central position in Western Civilization's approach to education. Originating as a body of knowledge that was essential for free citizens of ancient Greek city-states to execute their civic responsibilities, the liberal arts (or the arts of liberty), are considered the key to cultivating the well-rounded and virtuous citizenry essential to democratic rule and span a breadth of subjects traditionally including grammar, logic, rhetoric, arithmetic, geometry, music, and astronomy. From especially poetry, history, and oratory, the liberal arts developed, according to Cicero, "for the purpose of fashioning the minds of the young according to *humanitas* and virtue." Cicero, *De Oratore*, trans. E. W. Sutton and H. Rackham, Loeb Classical Library (Cambridge: Harvard University Press, 1942), 46. Throughout history, even into the twentieth century, a large body of writers from Thomas Aquinas, to Petrus Paulus Vergerius, to Mark Van Doren have described the central role of the liberal arts in forming independent citizens capable of self-governance. For additional reading see: John Henry Newman, *The Idea of a University* (1852 repr., Oxford University Press, 1976); Frederick Rudolph, *Curriculum: A History of the American Undergraduate Course of Study Since 1636* (Jossey-Bass, 1977); and Bruce Kimball, *Orators and Philosophers: A History of the Idea of Liberal Education* (Teachers College Press, 1986).

destroy us as civilized persons. It helps us see the world clearly and honestly. In revealing human nature, it reveals what is right and good for human beings: authentic education is not "value-neutral" but includes moral education that explains the standards for right and wrong. It takes up the hard but essential task of character formation. Such an education can form free men and free women—self-reliant and responsible persons capable of governing themselves as individuals and taking part in self-government.

Such an education starts by teaching that all Americans are equal members of one national community. The unique character and talents of each person should be recognized and developed. The wide experiences and the varied backgrounds of our citizens should be respected and honored. But the truths that equality and liberty belong by nature to every human being without exception must be taught as the moral basis of civic friendship, economic opportunity, citizenship, and political freedom.

Such an education respects students' intelligence and thirst for the truth. It is unafraid both to focus on the contributions made by the exceptional few, or acknowledge those that are less powerful, less fortunate, weaker, or marginalized. With the principle of equality as a foundation, such an education can incorporate the study of injustice and of tragedy in human affairs—including the American story's uglier parts—and patiently addresses the ways injustices can be corrected.

Rather than learning to hate one's country or the world for its inevitable wrongs, the well-educated student learns to appreciate and cherish the oases of civilization: solid family structures and local communities; effective, representative, and limited government; the rule of law and the security of civil rights and private property; a love of the natural world and the arts; good character and religious faith.

In the American context, an essential purpose of this honest approach is to encourage citizens to embrace and cultivate love of country. Thoughtful citizens embrace their national community not only because it is their own, but also because they see what it can be at its best. Just as students know their family members have good qualities and flaws, good education will reckon the depths and heights of our common history.

Genuine Civics Education

Civics and government classes should rely almost exclusively on primary sources. Primary sources link students with the real events and persons they are studying. The writings, speeches, first-hand accounts, and documents of those who were acting out the drama of history open a genuine communication, mediated by the written word, between historical figures and students that can bring to life the past. Primary sources without selective editing also allow students to study principles and arguments unfiltered by present-day historians' biases and agendas.

It is important for students to learn the reasons America's founders gave for building our country as they did. Students should learn and contemplate what the founders' purposes, hopes, and greatest concerns truly were, and primary sources will help them begin these considerations. Students should not read the Declaration of Independence as archaeology but as the idea that animates our nation with claims that are true for all time. As Alexander Hamilton reminds us in one of those primary documents (his 1775 essay *Farmer Refuted*),

The sacred rights of mankind are not to be rummaged for, among old parchments, or musty records. They are written, as with a sun beam, in the whole volume of human nature, by the hand of the divinity itself; and can never be erased or obscured by mortal power.[5]

Civics and government classes ought to teach students about the philosophical principles and foundations of the American republic, including natural law, natural rights, human equality, liberty, and constitutional self-government. Students should learn the reasons why our constitutional order is structured as a representative democracy and why a constitutional republic includes such features as the separation of powers, checks and balances, and federalism. They should study the benefits and achievements of our constitutional order, the Civil War's challenge to that order, and the ways the Constitution has been changed—not only by amendment and not always for the better—over the course of time. Finally, these classes ought to culminate in the student's understanding and embracing the responsibilities of good citizenship.

A genuine civics education focuses on fundamental questions concerning the American experiment in self-government. The best way to proceed is for the teacher to assign core original documents to students to read as carefully and thoroughly as they are able and then initiate age-appropriate discussion to surface and consider the meaning of the document. Teachers will find that students of every age have a genuine interest in engaging in discussion (and disagreement) about what these documents say, because they soon realize these enduring words speak to their own lives and experiences.

Using the Declaration of Independence, the Constitution, and the *Federalist Papers*, the following are a few examples of prompts teachers can use to encourage civics discussion amongst students :[6]

- What does human equality mean in the statement that "all men are created equal"? Equal in what respects? What view of human nature does this presuppose? Does the Declaration intend to include African Americans, as Abraham Lincoln, Frederick Douglass, and Martin Luther King, Jr., all insisted?

- What does the Declaration mean by asserting that all persons possess rights that are not "alienable"? Who or what, precisely, can alienate our rights? Are all rights deemed inalienable, or only some? And if the latter, why are they different?

- Why did the founding generation consider government's powers to be "just" only when government is instituted by the consent of the governed? Is justice for the founders based on nothing more than consent? What considerations might be more authoritative than consent?

- At the time the *Federalist Papers* were being written, the new Constitution did not include the Bill of Rights. What are the rights and protections enumerated in the Bill of Rights and how did they come to be amendments to the Constitution?

- Why did the founders opt for representative democracy

over the "pure" version of democracy practiced in ancient Athens? How do the two kinds of democracy differ? What did the *Federalist* assert was the inadequacy of ancient democracy?

- How does the Constitution seek to reconcile democracy, which means rule by the majority, with the rights of minorities? Stated differently, how does the Constitution do justice both to the equality of all and to the liberty of each? What exactly is the difference between a democracy and republic?

- What economic conditions make American democracy possible? Could American democracy under the Constitution be reconciled with any and every economic system? Why does the Constitution protect property rights? Why do critics of American democracy such as Karl Marx believe that private property (protected by our Constitution) is the root of injustice? How would Madison and Hamilton have responded to Marx and his followers' criticisms?

- Students should read the best-known speeches and writings of progressive presidents Woodrow Wilson, Theodore Roosevelt, and Franklin Roosevelt on economic democracy. In what ways do they differ from the principles and structure of the Constitution? Would the Constitution need to be significantly amended to fit their proposals? Apart from amendments, in what other ways has progressivism changed our constitutional system?

- Implicit in these questions are other basic documents and major speeches that every American citizen should study. The questions concerning the meaning of human equality, inalienable rights, popular consent, and the right of revolution call for a fresh examination—in the light of the Declaration—of such key works as Frederick Douglass's speech on "The Meaning of the Fourth of July to the Negro" and Chief Justice Taney's infamous opinion for the Supreme Court majority in *Dred Scott v. Sandford* (holding that African-Americans "had no rights which the white man was bound to respect"). Douglass's and Lincoln's scathing criticisms of Taney's pro-slavery opinion should be taught with these as well.

- Students should read the 1848 Seneca Falls "Declaration of Sentiments and Resolutions" calling for women's suffrage, and Dr. Martin Luther King, Jr.'s "I Have a Dream" speech. Why did Elizabeth Cady Stanton look to the form and substance of the Declaration of Independence in crafting the Seneca Falls Declaration? What did King mean in asserting that the Declaration of Independence and the Constitution constituted a "promissory note to which every American was to fall heir"?

These questions cover just a sample of the issues that come to the fore as students read the primary documents of the founding and history of America. Other less fundamental but still important documents, speeches, and topics could be added. Recognizing that political activism has no place in formal education, mock civics and community service projects should be encouraged.

Conclusion

Among the virtues to be cultivated in the American republic, the founders knew that a free people must have a knowledge of the principles and practices of liberty, and an appreciation of their origins and challenges.

While this country has its imperfections, just like any other country, in the annals of history the United States has achieved the greatest degree of personal freedom, security, and prosperity for the greatest proportion of its own people and for others around the world. These results are the good fruit of the ideas the founding generation expressed as true for all people at all times and places.

An authentic civics education will help rebuild our common bonds, our mutual friendship, and our civic devotion. But we cannot *love* what we do not *know*.

This is why civics education, education relating to the citizen, must begin with knowledge, which is, as George Washington reminds us, "the surest basis of public happiness."[7]

ENDNOTES

I. INTRODUCTION

1. Executive Order 13958, 85 Fed. Reg. 70951 (Nov. 2, 2020), which created the President's Advisory 1776 Commission.

2. Abraham Lincoln, "Letter to Henry L. Pierce and Others," in *The Collected Works of Abraham Lincoln*, ed. Roy P. Basler, vol. 3 (New Brunswick: Rutgers University Press, 1990), 375. This quotation was corrected from the original.

3. Abraham Lincoln, "Speech at Springfield, Illinois, June 26,1857," in *The Collected Works of Abraham Lincoln*, ed. Roy P. Basler, vol. 2 (New Brunswick: Rutgers University Press, 1990), 406.

II. THE MEANING OF THE DECLARATION

1. Abraham Lincoln, "Letter to Henry L. Pierce and Others," in *The Collected Works of Abraham Lincoln*, ed. Roy P. Basler, vol. 3 (New Brunswick: Rutgers University Press, 1990), 375.

2. Alexander Hamilton et al., "Federalist 2," in *The Federalist Papers*, ed. Clinton Rossiter (New York, NY: Mentor, 1999), 32.

3. Thomas Jefferson, "Letter to Roger C. Weightman," in Writings, ed. Merrill D. Peterson (New York, NY: The Library of America, 2011), 1517. Jefferson is paraphrasing from Algernon Sidney, "The Liberty of a People Is the Gift of God and Nature," in *Discourses Concerning Government*, ed. Thomas G. West (Indianapolis: Liberty Fund, 1996), 511.

4. Abraham Lincoln, "Letter to Henry L. Pierce and Others," in *The Collected Works of Abraham Lincoln*, ed. Roy P. Basler, vol. 3 (New Brunswick, NJ: Rutgers University Press, 1990), 376.

III. A CONSTITUTION OF PRINCIPLES

1. On the relationship between the Declaration of Independence and the Constitution, see Larry P. Arnn, *The Founders' Key: The Divine and Natural Connection Between the Declaration and the Constitution and What We Risk by Losing It* (Nashville: Thomas Nelson, 2012) and on the principles of the Declaration and the Constitution, Matthew Spalding, *We Still Hold These Truths: Rediscovering Our Principles, Reclaiming Our Future* (Wilmington: ISI Books, 2009).

2. Thomas Paine, *The Life and Works of Thomas Paine*, ed. William M. Van der Weyde (New Rochelle, NY: Thomas Paine National Historical Association, 1925), 147-148.

3. Abraham Lincoln, "Fragment on the Constitution and the Union," in *The Collected Works of Abraham Lincoln*, ed. Roy P. Basler, vol. 4 (New Brunswick: Rutgers University Press, 1990), 169.

4. Alexander Hamilton et al., "Federalist 47," in *The Federalist Papers*, ed. Clinton Rossiter (New York, NY: Mentor, 1999), 298.

5. Alexander Hamilton et al., "Federalist 10," in *The Federalist Papers*, ed. Clinton Rossiter (New York, NY: Mentor, 1999), 76.

IV. CHALLENGES TO AMERICA'S PRINCIPLES

1. George Washington, "Farewell Address," in *The Papers of George Washington*, vol. 20 (Charlottesville, VA: University of Virginia Press, 2019), 709.

2. See David Brion Davis, *The Problem of Slavery in Western Culture* (New York: Oxford University Press, 1966) and *The Problem of Slavery in the Age of Revolution 1770-1823* (New York: Oxford University Press, 1999).

3. In general, see Sean Wilentz, *No Property in Man: Slavery and Antislavery at the Nation's Founding* (Cambridge: Harvard University Press, 2018), as well as Bernard Bailyn, *Ideological Origins of the American Revolution* (Cambridge, MA: Belknap Press of Harvard University Press, 1987), 232-246 and Paul Rahe, *Republics Ancient and Modern* (Chapel Hill, NC: University of North Carolina Press, 1992), 617-641.

4. George Washington, "Letter to Robert Morris," in *The Papers of George Washington*, vol. 4 (Charlottesville, VA: University Press of Virginia, 1995), 16.

5. "He has waged cruel war against human nature itself, violating it's most sacred rights of life and liberty in the persons of a distant people who never offended him, captivating & carrying them into slavery in another hemisphere, or to incur miserable death in their transportation thither. This piratical warfare, the opprobium of INFIDEL powers, is the warfare of the CHRISTIAN king of Great Britain. Determined to keep open a market where MEN should be bought & sold, he has prostituted his negative for suppressing every legislative attempt to prohibit or to restrain this execrable commerce. And that this assemblage of horrors might want no fact of distinguished die, he is now exciting those very people to rise in arms among us, and to purchase that liberty of which he has deprived them, by murdering the people on whom he also obtruded them: thus paying off former crimes committed against the LIBERTIES of one people, with crimes which he urges them to commit against the LIVES of another." Thomas Jefferson, "A Declaration by the Representatives of the United States of America, in General Congress Assembled" in *Writings*, ed. Merrill D. Peterson (New York, NY: The Library of America, 2011), 22.

6. Thomas Jefferson, "Notes on the State of Virginia: Query XVIII," in *Writings*, ed. Merrill D. Peterson (New York, NY: The Library of America, 2011), 289.

7. James Madison, *The Records of the Federal Convention of 1787*, vol. 2, ed. Max Farrand (New Haven, CT: Yale University Press), 417.

8. *Journals of the Continental Congress*, 1774-1789, ed. Worthington C.

Ford et al. (Washington, D.C., 1904-37), 1:77 and 4:258.

9. "An Ordinance for the Government of the Territory of the United States Northwest of the River Ohio, Art. 6," in *Journals of the Continental Congress: 1774-1789*, ed. Worthington Chauncey Ford, vol. 32 (Washington: Government Print. Office, 1906), 334-343.

10. Abraham Lincoln, "Speech on the Dred Scott Decision June 26, 1857," in *The Collected Works of Abraham Lincoln*, ed. Roy P. Basler, vol. 2 (New Brunswick, NJ: Rutgers University Press, 1990), 406.

11. John Adams, "Letter to Joseph Ward, 8 January 1810," in John Adams, *Writings from the New Nation, 1784-1826*, ed. Gordon S. Wood (New York, NY: Library of America, 2016), 517. And John Adams to William Tudor, Jr., 20 November 1819," *Founders Online*, National Archives, https://founders.archives.gov/documents/ Adams/99-02-02-7261.

12. Frederick Douglass, "'What to the Slave Is the Fourth of July?" in Frederick Douglass, *The Essential Douglass: Selected Writings & Speeches*, ed. Nicholas Buccola (Indianapolis, Indiana: Hackett Publishing Company Inc., 2016), 53, 69.

13. John C. Calhoun, "Speech on the Oregon Bill," in *Union and Liberty: The Political Philosophy of John C. Calhoun*, ed. Ross M. Lence (Indianapolis, IN: Liberty Fund Inc, 1992), 569. It was Senator John Pettit who referred to the Declaration as a self-evident lie (February 20, 1854, 33th Cong., 1st Session, Congressional Globe, 214). Calhoun also wrote that "These great and dangerous errors have their origin in the prevalent opinion that all men are born free and equal—than which nothing can be more unfounded and false." John. C. Calhoun, *A Disquisition on Government* (1853) in Union and Liberty (Indianapolis, IN: Liberty Fund, 2014), 44.

14. John C. Calhoun, "Speech on the Reception of Abolition Petitions," in *Union and Liberty: The Political Philosophy of John C. Calhoun*, ed. Ross M. Lence (Indianapolis, IN: Liberty Fund, 1992), 474.

15. Abraham Lincoln, "Third Debate with Stephen A. Douglas at Jonesboro, Illinois," in *The Collected Works of Abraham Lincoln*, ed. Roy P. Basler, vol. 3 (New Brunswick, NJ: Rutgers Univ. Press, 1990), 117.

16. The Civil War resolved the question of slavery through Lincoln's wartime issuance of the Emancipation Proclamation and then the Thirteenth Amendment. On Lincoln, slavery, and emancipation, see Harry V. Jaffa, *A New Birth of Freedom: Abraham Lincoln and the Coming of the Civil War* (Lanham: Rowman & Littlefield Publishers, 2000), Allen C. Guelzo, *Lincoln's Emancipation Proclamation: The End of Slavery in America* (New York: Simon & Schuster, 2004) and James Oakes, *The Crooked Path to Abolition: Abraham Lincoln and the Antislavery Constitution* (W.W. Norton & Company, 2021).

17. Carl L. Becker, *The Declaration of Independence: A Study in the History of Political Ideas* (Alfred A. Knopf Inc., 1942), 277. The book was first published in 1922.

18. Woodrow Wilson lays out the theory of the modern state in "The Study of Administration," *Political Science Quarterly* 2, no. 2 (June 1887): 197-222. On Wilson, see Ronald Pestritto, *Woodrow Wilson and the Roots of Modern Liberalism* (Lanham: Roman & Littlefield Publishers, 2005). See also Thomas C. Leonard, *Illiberal Reformers: Race, Eugenics, and American Economics in the Progressive Era* (Princeton, NJ: Princeton University Press, 2016). Philip Hamburger, in his *Is Administrative Law Unlawful?* (Chicago: The University of Chicago Press, 2014), argues that administrative law is in essence a return to the kind of absolutist prerogative power exercised by the English Crown. The Framers of the Constitution, however, drew on a tradition of constitutionalism that "developed precisely to bar this sort of consolidated extra- and supra-legal power" (494). Indeed, Hamburger argues, Americans went further than their English predecessors in formulating a view of constitutionalism that "made clear that not only their executives but even their legislators were without absolute power" (ibid.).

19. Benito Mussolini, "Speech before the Chamber of Deputies," in *Discorsi Del* 1928 (Milano: Casa Editrice "Alpes", 1929), 157.

20. Franklin Delano Roosevelt, "Radio Address Delivered by President From Washington, December 29, 1940," in *Peace and War: United States Foreign Policy, 1931-1941* (Washington, D.C.: U.S., Government Printing Office, 1943), 603.

21. Karl Marx and Friedrich Engels, Letter to August Bebel, Wilhelm Liebknecht, Wilhelm Brache and Others. "Strategy and Tactics of the Class Struggle, September 17, 1879," in *Collected Works of Karl Marx, Frederick Engels*, vol. 45 (International Publishers, 1975), 394-408.

22. Karl Marx, "Letter to J. Weydemeyer, March 5, 1852," in *Marx & Engels Collected Works*, vol. 39 (Lawrence & Wishart, 2010), 62-5.

23. Friedrich Engels and Karl Marx, *Manifesto of the Communist Party* (New York, NY: International Publishers, 1989), 44.

24. Ronald Reagan, "Remarks to the People of Foreign Nations on New Year's Day January 1, 1982," in *Public Papers of the Presidents of the United States*, vol. 1 (Washington, D.C.: U.S. Govt. Print. Off., 1983), 2.

25. For a brief history of the policy failure of reconstruction, see Allen Guelzo, *Reconstruction: A Concise History* (Oxford University Press, 2018). In particular, see C. Vann Woodward, *The Strange Career of Jim Crow* (Oxford University Press, 1966) 2nd revised edition. Woodward argues that segregation in the South dates to the 1890s when Jim Crow laws divided the races more than previously under slavery. Originally published in 1955, the author's revised edition enlarges the discussion to include the early Civil Rights movement. See also Carol Swain, *Black Face, Black Interests: The Representation of African Americans in Congress* (Cambridge: Harvard University Press, 1993).

26. Martin Luther King, "I Have a Dream speech (1963)," in *A Testament of Hope: The Essential Writings and Speeches* ed. James Melvin Washington (New York, NY: HarperCollins Publishers, 1991), 217-220.

27. "Civil rights laws were not passed to give civil rights protection to all Americans, as the majority of this Commission seems to believe. Instead, they were passed out of a recognition that some Americans already had protection because they belonged to a favored group; and others, including blacks, Hispanics, and women of all races, did not because they belonged to disfavored groups. If we are ever to achieve the real equality of opportunity that is the bright

hope and promise of America, we must not deny our history and present condition by substituting illusion for reality." Statement of Commissioners Blandina Cardenas Ramirez and Mary Frances Berry, *Toward an Understanding of Stotts* (U.S. Commission on Civil Rights: Clearinghouse Publications 85, January 1985), 63.

28. Martin Luther King, "I Have a Dream speech (1963)," in *A Testament of Hope: The Essential Writings and Speeches* ed. James Melvin Washington (New York, NY: HarperCollins Publishers, 1991), 217-220. See also Carol Swain, *The New White Nationalism in America: Its Challenge to Integration* (New York: Cambridge University Press, 2002).

V. THE TASK OF NATIONAL RENEWAL

1. Cf., Wilfred M. McClay, "Civic Education, Rightly Understood," *City Journal*, Spring 2021, forthcoming.

2. James Wilson, "On the Study of the Law in the United States," James Wilson, *The Works of James Wilson*, ed. Robert Green McCloskey, vol. 1, (Cambridge, Massachusetts: Belknap Press of Harvard University Press, 1967), 72.

3. Thomas Jefferson, "Letter to Henry Lee," in *Writings*, ed. Merrill D. Peterson (New York, NY: The Library of America, 2011), 1501.

4. John Adams, "To the Inhabitants of the Colony of Massachusetts-Bay," in *Papers of John Adams* (Cambridge, MA: Harvard Univ. Pr., 1977), 307-327.

5. Abraham Lincoln, "Address Before the Young Men's Lyceum of Springfield, Illinois," in *The Collected Works of Abraham Lincoln*, ed. Roy P. Balser, vol. 1 (New Brunswick: Rutgers University Press, 1990), 108-12.

VI. CONCLUSION

1. Calvin Coolidge, "Speech on the 150th Anniversary of the Declaration of Independence, July 5, 1926" in *Foundations of the Republic:*

Speeches and Addresses, ed. Robert J. Taylor (New York: Scribner, 1926), 451.

APPENDIX II
FAITH AND AMERICA'S PRINCIPLES

1. Thomas Jefferson, "'Draft of Instructions to the Virginia Delegates in the Continental Congress,'" in *The Papers of Thomas Jefferson*, vol. 1 (Princeton, NJ: Princeton University Press, 1950), 121-137.

2. George Washington, "Farewell Address," in *The Papers of George Washington*, vol. 20, ed. Jennifer E. Streenshorne (Charlottesville: University of Virginia Press, 2019), 712.

3. See Brian Tierney, *The Crisis of Church and State 1050-1300* (1964; repr., Toronto: University of Toronto Press, 1988), esp. Part I, The First Thousand Years; and Harold J. Berman, *Law and Revolution: The Formation of the Western Legal Tradition* (Cambridge, MA: Harvard University Press, 1983), esp. ch. 2, The Origin of the Western Legal Tradition in the Papal Revolution.

4. A detailed history of how the founders' idea of religious liberty or 'separation of church and state' was transformed into an entirely different notion of complete separation of religion from politics can be found in Philip Hamburger, *Separation of Church and State* (Cambridge, MA: Harvard University Press, 2002). See also Vincent Phillip Muñoz, *God and the Founders: Madison, Washington, and Jefferson* (Cambridge University Press, 2009).

5. Samuel Cooper, "A Sermon on the Commencement of the Constitution, October 25, 1780" in *Political Sermons of the American Founding Era, 1730-1805*, ed. Ellis Sandoz, vol. 1 (Indianapolis, IN: Liberty Fund, 1998), 637.

6. Calvin Coolidge, "Speech on the 150th Anniversary of the Declaration of Independence, July 5, 1926" in *Foundations of the Republic: Speeches and Addresses* (New York: Scribner, 1926), 450.

7. *American Antislavery Writings: Colonial Beginnings to Emancipation*, ed. James G. Baker (New York: Library of America, 2012), 4, 567.

8. George Washington, "Letter to the Hebrew Congregation in Newport, Rhode Island, 18 August 1790," in *The Papers of George Washington*, Presidential Series, ed. Mark A. Mastromarino, vol. 6 (Charlottesville: University Press of Virginia, 1996), 285.

APPENDIX III
CREATED EQUAL OR IDENTITY POLITICS?

1. Abraham Lincoln, Speech of July 10, 1858, in *The Collected Works of Abraham Lincoln*, ed. Roy P. Basler, vol. 2 (New Brunswick: Rutgers University Press, 1990), 500.

2. Antonio Gramsci, *Selections from the Prison Notebooks of Antonio Gramsci*, ed. Quintin Hoare and Geoffrey Navell Smith (Lawrence & Wishart, 1971), 5-23.

3. Herbert Marcuse, *One Dimensional Man Studies in the Ideology of Advanced Industrial Society* (Boston: Beacon Press, 1964), 256.

4. An influential essay in critical race theory, which introduced the now widely-used term "intersectionality," is Kimberlé Crenshaw, "Demarginalizing the Intersection of Race and Sex: A Black Feminist Critique of Antidiscrimination Doctrine, Feminist Theory and Antiracist Politics," University of Chicago Legal Forum 1:8 (1989). For two important works advocating critical race theory in America, see Mari Matsuda, Charles R. Lawrence III, Richard Delgado, and Kimberle Williams Crenshaw *Words That Wound: Critical Race Theory, Assaultive Speech, And The First Amendment* (Westview Press, 1993) and Richard Delgado and Jean Stefancic, *Critical Race Theory: An Introduction* (New York: New York University Press, 2017).

5. Martin Luther King, "I Have a Dream speech (1963)," in *A Testament of Hope: The Essential Writings and Speeches* ed. James Melvin Washington (New York, NY: HarperCollins Publishers, 1991), 217-220.

6. Cf., Shulamith Firestone, *The Dialectic of Sex: The Case for Feminist Revolution* (William Morrow and Company, 1970) and Stokely Carmichael and Charles V. Hamilton, *Black Power: The Politics of*

Liberation (New York: Random House, 1967). In response, consider Arthur M. Schlesinger's critique *Disuniting of America: Reflections on a Multicultural Society* (Knoxville, TN: Whittle Books, 1991) and more recently *Mike Gonzalez, The Plot to Change America: How Identity Politics is Dividing the Land of the Free* (New York: Encounter Books, 2020).

7. Cf., the Executive Order that abolishes the 1776 Commission at the same time that it favors aggregating Americans "by race, ethnicity, gender, disability, income, veteran status, or other key demographic variables" in order to measure and advance an equity agenda. Exec. Order 13985, 86 Fed. Reg. 7009 (Jan. 20, 2021).

8. Abraham Lincoln, "Letter to Henry L. Pierce and Others," in *The Collected Works of Abraham Lincoln*, ed. Roy P. Basler, vol. 3 (New Brunswick: Rutgers University Press, 1990), 375.

APPENDIX IV:
TEACHING AMERICANS ABOUT THEIR COUNTRY

1. James Madison, "Letter to William T. Barry" August 4, 1822 in *The Papers of James Madison*, Retirement Series, vol. 2, 1 February 1820–26 February 1823, ed. David B. Mattern, J. C. A. Stagg, Mary Parke Johnson, and Anne Mandeville Colony (Charlottesville: University of Virginia Press, 2013), 557.

2. Abraham Lincoln, "Speech on the Dred Scott Decision June 26, 1857," in *The Collected Works of Abraham Lincoln*, ed. Roy P. Basler, vol. 2 (New Brunswick, NJ: Rutgers University Press, 1990), 406.

3. See Peter Wood, ed., *Drilling through the Core: Why Common Core is Bad for America* (Pioneer Institute, 2015) and *Common Core: Yea & Nay* (Encounter Broadside, 2014)

4. See David Randall, "Making Citizens: How American Universities Teach Civics," National Association of Scholars, January 2017, available at: https://www.nas.org/storage/app/media/Reports/Making%20Citizens/NAS_makingCitizens_fullReport.pdf

5. Alexander Hamilton, "The Farmer Refuted," in *The Papers of*

Alexander Hamilton, ed. Harold C Syrett (New York: Columbia Univ. Press, 1961), 122.

6. These examples were adapted by the author of Thomas K. Lindsay, "Becoming American," Inside Higher Ed, April 25, 2008, https:// www.insidehighered.com/views/2008/04/25/becoming-american.

7. George Washington, "First Annual Message to Congress," in *The Papers of George Washington*, Presidential Series, vol. 4, 8 September 1789–15 January 1790, ed. Dorothy Twohig (Charlottesville: University Press of Virginia, 1993), 545.

The President's Advisory 1776 Commission

Larry P. Arnn, Chair
Carol Swain, Vice Chair
Matthew Spalding, Executive Director

Phil Bryant • Jerry Davis • Michael Farris
Gay Hart Gaines • John Gibbs • Mike Gonzalez
Victor Davis Hanson • Charles Kesler • Peter Kirsanow
Thomas Lindsay • Bob McEwen • Ned Ryun • Julie Strauss

Ex-officio Members
Michael Pompeo, Secretary of State
Christopher C. Miller, Acting Secretary of Defense
David L. Bernhardt, Secretary of the Interior
Ben Carson, Secretary of Housing and Urban Development
Mitchell M. Zais, Acting Secretary of Education
Brooke Rollins, Assistant to the President for Domestic Policy
Doug Hoelscher, Assistant to the President for Intergovernmental Affairs

The Commission is grateful to the following individuals who assisted
with the preparation of *The 1776 Report*:
William Bock, Alexandra Campana, Ariella Campana, Joshua Charles,
Emily Weston Kannon, Brian Morgenstern, Macy Mount,
Elise Robinson, McKenzie Snow, and Alec Torres.